Celtic
Sex Magic

Celtic
Sex Magic

For Couples, Groups, and
Solitary Practitioners

JON G. HUGHES

Destiny Books
Rochester, Vermont

Destiny Books
One Park Street
Rochester, Vermont 05767
www.InnerTraditions.com

Destiny Books is a division of Inner Traditions International

Copyright © 2001 by Jon G. Hughes

Library of Congress Cataloging-in-Publication Data

Hughes, Jon G., 1951-
   Celtic sex magic : for couples, groups, and solitary practitioners /
Jon G. Hughes.
      p. cm.
   ISBN 0-89281-908-1
   1. Magic. 2. Sex. 3. Magic, Celtic.   I. Title.
   BF1623.S4 H84 2001
   133.4'3'089916—dc21
                              2001003486

Printed and bound in Italy

10 9 8 7 6 5 4 3 2 1

This book was typeset in Cheltenham, with American Uncial and Aon Cari as display typefaces

I would like to dedicate this book to my wife, Yve, upon whose love and support I depend entirely. Also to Livingstone, Morgan, Molly, Mulligan, Montgomery, and Oliver, who provide us both with never-ending affection and inspiration.

Contents

Part 2:

How the Sex Magic Ritual Works

Part 3:
Performing Workings and Rituals

Acknowledgments

I would like to extend my grateful thanks to the following, whose invaluable help at various critical stages in the writing of this book made it both possible and enjoyable:

Vincent O'Shea, whose photographic and artistic input proved crucial. May his many talents continue to be recognized and utilized.

Eoghan, Linda, and Tienne for their cooperation in the early stages of the book's development.

Marie, Theresa, Sam, Nathan, and Pat, whose assistance was readily given.

Liz-Ann, for her help in the organization of much of the practical work of this book.

Introduction

This is not yet another history of the Celts and the Druids, nor is it another romanticized retelling of Celtic beliefs and Druidic wizardry. You'll find here no ancient gods and no heroic myths. This book concerns itself with the practical working of Celtic sex magic: the ritualized preparation, focus, and release of the immense natural energy produced by sexual orgasm. In Druidic tradition, this energy is used to empower and cast spells for the betterment of individuals and of society in general.

This ritual is not recreated from ancient texts but has been perpetuated through an oral tradition, handed down to me through seven generations of a family lineage of Druids. To my knowledge little, if any, record of this ritual has been previously documented.

Our journey begins with an introduction to Druidic tradition, including how Druidic practices and rituals are handed down through generations, using my personal experience as a reference. We'll then review the basic concepts and equipment necessary to embark on the study and practice of sex magic.

It continues with an exploration of the methods of focusing, channeling, and projecting personal energy through the explosive intensity of the sexual orgasm.

It concludes with a detailed look at rituals, workings, and practices that will allow you to begin your own adventure with Celtic sex magic.

Although there has been a resurgence of interest in Celtic culture and philosophy over the past decade, the sex magic ritual has been generally ignored; some see it as distasteful, others see it as a threat to Christian morality, and still others fear it as a dangerous perversion. Few understand its purpose, the immense fulfillment it can bring to its participants, or the potency of its influences. For me this book begins a personal quest: the validation of this authentic and legitimate Druidic practice.

PART 1:
The Journey Begins

Passing on the Tradition

"And so it begins . . ."

I thought that for me it began at the age of twelve, but looking back now I can see that it probably began on the day I was born, if not before.

Through the ages, the Druidic tradition has been passed on from father to chosen son, or from mother to chosen daughter. On rare occasions, a non-family apprentice is chosen to enter the tradition. The relationship of giver to receiver is less important than the concept that the receiver is "chosen."

My family genealogy provides me with a mix of Celtic blood. My paternal lineage is Welsh for at least six generations, while my maternal lineage is Scottish for a known five generations. Having been born and raised in a small Welsh village, the Welsh side of my cultural heritage has inevitably been the stronger.

I was to learn that my grandfather was the latest in a long family line of Druids. The verbal tradition he inherited described a lineage stretching back at least five generations, to a time when the entire Welsh valley in which we lived was an agricultural settlement. Small farms and cottages covered the area that was, by the time I was born, a predominantly late-Victorian coal-mining village.

Fortunately, because of the way the Welsh valleys were developed during the Industrial Revolution, the bulk of the commercial and industrial development was, and still is, focused within the base of the valley. The majority of the residential properties, in the form of terraced miners' cottages, occupy the mid-section of the valley sides, leaving the uppermost part of the valleys, the sides of the mountains forming the valleys, still in the hands of the small farmers and the National Parks Authority.

This meant that, although I was brought up in a small miner's cottage, in the midst of a bleak coal-mining community, I was never far from the fields and woodland that enchanted me for the whole of my youth. It was, in fact, while walking in the local woodland with my grandfather, on what I seem to remember was a bright summer day, that my journey into the tradition began.

It was not unusual for my grandfather, my brother, and me to venture out into the woods, but on this occasion it was just my grandfather and me. I wasn't aware of it at the time, but what I was listening to as we walked along was not just a fairy story about the trees, rocks, and plants around us. It was the beginning of a ten-year period of training in an oral tradition that was to result in my initiation as a Druid at the age of twenty-two.

It was a great frustration to my grandfather that he was not able to see a successor for his Druidic craft in either of his two sons. This may well have been because both were called to fight in the Second World War; both survived, but his younger son never returned to Wales, while his elder son, my father, returned with a young bride and his own plans for the future in post-war Wales.

My grandfather told me many years later that before I was born he felt a reassurance that I would be a male child and the inheritor of his knowledge of the Druidic traditions. During my younger years he saw in me what he later called a "spiritual peace," which he felt sure would make me a worthy vessel for the tradition.

I became my grandfather's "chosen" successor.

My Druidic Education

By my late teens, I had been inaugurated into many of the practices and rituals of the Welsh Druidic tradition. As a result of my particular interest in herbal healing and even greater interest in the secrets of making, cleansing, and energizing Celtic wands, I had reached a point where my grandfather was finding it difficult to maintain a flow of new and stimulating information to feed my growing appetite.

It was at this point that, for the first time in all of my training, I was made aware that there were other Druidic practitioners in our own community.

Over the next four years I became deeply involved with five other practitioners,

all from within our small mining community. Three of these were, like myself, learning the tradition; another was then a middle-aged priestess; and the last was an older Druid, probably around sixty-five at the time, who in hindsight was undoubtedly one of the great influences in my Druidic development.

For the following three years my main study was divided between the secrets of wand making with the Druid elder and the role of Celtic sex magic as taught to another apprentice and me by the Druidic priestess.

Since those early days, some thirty years ago now, I have continued in the role that was destined for me. My learning continues each day as my spirituality grows. I am still on the infinite path of knowledge and now spend a great deal of my time in research and practicing my given arts. Though I keep in touch with all the crafts and traditions I have been endowed with, my main focus is without doubt still my lifelong fascination with the making and energizing of Celtic wands and with Celtic sex magic.

Secrets Revealed

I was surprised to be introduced to other Druidic practitioners in my community, which suggests that there was, and still is, an element of secrecy to the Druidic tradition. This is inevitably the case. When one considers the history of cultural and religious suppression in Wales (as in Ireland and Scotland) by the occupying English landowners and industrialists, it is surprising that any traditions survived. The Welsh language itself was very nearly lost, as were the other Celtic and Gaelic tongues. Paganism was suppressed to the point of official extinction. As early as the Roman invasion, Druidism was outlawed, with the exception of the Bardic practice; other Druidic practices went underground.

In Wales, concealing Druidic practice was relatively easy, as Welsh people are by nature reserved and have a strong sense of community; those in need turn to their friends and neighbors for support and help. It is not easy to keep a secret within a small Welsh village, but once the community knows, it keeps the secret to itself. In this way, Welsh Druid practitioners were and remain always available to their communities, but to outsiders they are invisible.

The one-to-one relationship of Druid and student forms the basis of the maintenance of the oral tradition. The Druidic priest (or priestess) devises a unique training methodology to best suit each student he or she initiates.

Only as a result of this unusual quirk in the collective Welsh personality has the Druidic tradition survived. I can vouch for this personally, having been both a Druidic practitioner and a member of one of those small Welsh communities; I have been a keeper of both secrets.

Although the Druidic practitioner is an integral part of the community, he or she is the possessor of what could be deemed "secret" knowledge. In the same way that medical doctors, surgeons, lawyers, and other professional practitioners are privy to certain knowledge and practices relating to their profession that, in other, less knowledgeable hands, could be misused, so the Druidic priest or priestess is privy to knowledge and practices that are necessary for the application of his or her skills.

Secrecy does create a division, rightly or wrongly, between those who know and those who do not, but consider this: A true Druidic practitioner is the leader of a group of pagan followers. The belief system they pursue is paganism, not Druidism. The Druid is, and always has been, the trained, experienced holder of a wealth of knowledge relating to the pagan belief system. Without this specific knowledge the belief system could be (and in the past has been) distorted and corrupted.

There are two main reasons why the "secrets" of the tradition are limited to the Druid and his or her chosen successor. The first is deeply enthroned in the Druidic ethos and is illustrated in greater detail in the later section of the book describing the naming process. It is the belief that a Druid must fully understand the entirety of any concept or material thing before invoking the power of its name. In other words, to know the name of something is to have power over it. This belief is shared by a number of native belief systems throughout the world, including some North American native tribes.

In the context of learning the Druidic tradition this concept means that before Druid students practice their knowledge unsupervised, they should be fully aware of the impact and ramifications of their actions and how the results of these actions may in turn affect other aspects of the tradition. This is why the training of a Druid is split into a number of "Ages" or training periods, sometimes mistakenly translated as years. Each Age or period focuses on a more or less self-contained area of the tradition (other than the first two periods, which are general in their nature). This means that as the student progresses and becomes

initiated into each progressive Age, he or she is effectively graduating from one complete area of knowledge to another—each time having a complete understanding of the previous area before being allowed to move forward into the next.

Without careful guidance and supervision to ensure that the student has mastered an Age, there exists a very real danger that may be summarized in the maxim "A little knowledge is a dangerous thing." Unless the student has achieved a full understanding of all the relationships and complexities of the given area of study, incomplete pieces of information may be used in isolation and out of context and then interpreted into a meaning that is a long way removed from its original intent.

The second reason why intricate details of Druidic practices are known by only a few is that the Druidic tradition that we know today is the product of generations of personal training and learning by Druidic Master and student. Usually both are members of the same extended family and live within the same community. Training is given through a unique personal dialog and by practical example, presented in a way particularly designed to suit the individual needs and abilities of the student concerned. Nothing is standardized, nothing is written down. The tradition remains an oral one, changed and adapted to the generation and times in which it is being applied, passed along on a one-to-one basis.

My own experience as a student was that my interest and enthusiasm for learning the tradition ebbed and flowed throughout my training period. Particularly as a mid- to late-teenager, when, as for other youngsters of my own age, my interests were developing elsewhere. My teachers at the time understood this and planned my training accordingly, changing the content of my training in order that I could relate it to the emotions and interests that were in the forefront of my thinking at the time.

My situation was in no way unique. In order for each student to receive "complete packages" of knowledge, each training is especially adapted to suit a student's individual needs. This kind of customized training is both time consuming and extremely demanding of both teacher and student, and while it does not prevent a Druid priest or priestess from having more than one student, it does mean that the time constraints involved in training each student individually prevents him or her from having more than a small number.

It is understandable then that by adhering to these principles and practices of Druidic training the knowledge of the tradition has not been, nor could it be, dispersed among the many.

One could indeed argue that without adequate training and instruction the bulk of the information considered to be secret would be at best meaningless and at worst very dangerous in unskilled hands. This is particularly relevant to sex magic. Unfortunately, these practices have been suppressed and vilified by modern society and misinterpreted by popular media as satanic rites and the domain of the sexually perverted. With this in mind, we must prepare ourselves with great care and attention to detail if we are to practice these crafts with focus and honesty; otherwise we are just furthering the argument of their misuse, and we must question our motivation for wanting to learn them.

In order to make this book of interest only to the sincere seeker of the knowledge it contains, I have deliberately presented all the illustrations, sexual practices, and rituals in a very straightforward form. They are certainly not designed for arousal and will hopefully deter any unwanted voyeur interest.

By now you may want to ask of me, "Aren't you breaking your oath of secrecy by disclosing the information in this book?"

The short answer is no.

Oaths are taken at initiation, at the point of progressing from one Age to another, and at the point where the Druid teacher believes that the student has absorbed all the knowledge he or she is able to pass on. This may mean that the student's training is complete or that the next stage of training is to be taken on by another teacher.

Each oath is related to the knowledge contained in the student's last Age of learning. The oaths are not related to "keeping the secrets" as in secret organizations like the Free Masons, but to how the knowledge and techniques are to be applied and to how the knowledge is to be passed on in the "complete" form as described above. It is in this context that I believe that I have not compromised or contradicted any of the oaths I have taken.

The Question of Translation

As you might expect, most if not all of the language associated with the Celtic sex magic ritual is Welsh in origin. The Welsh language, when spoken by a Welsh person, is uniquely lyrical and melodic and contains nuances both in meaning and in spirit that are difficult to translate into other languages without some loss of accuracy and sincerity.

However, I have deliberately avoided using any Welsh in this book. Instead, I have tried to capture in English the meaningful spirit of what is intended by the Welsh text, without burdening the reader with unfamiliar Welsh words.

I believe it is far better for the practitioner to use his or her mother tongue and to fully understand the intention and meaning of what is being said than to use Welsh or any other Celtic language simply to make the ritual sound exotic. Words that practitioners do not fully understand are meaningless and hollow when they are used in rituals.

"Modernizing" the Druidic rituals by translating them into English does not break from Druidic tradition. It is Druidic tradition to cherish the knowledge and practices of the past, and to use that understanding to maintain the meaningfulness of what is being practiced in the present day. Whatever new knowledge becomes available that is compatible with the Druidic fundamental belief system is absorbed into the tradition. The main reason Druidic rituals and practices appear to contain only ancient knowledge is that they have been suppressed and alien to society for so long that no one has seen their continued development. It can be argued, therefore, that the translation of these ancient Welsh texts into contemporary English, with no loss of meaning or intent, is wholly compatible with Druidic beliefs.

Accounting for Morality and the Law

If, like myself, you are living in a modern, western Christian society (Roman Catholicism is the "official" religion of the Republic of Ireland), you will find, as I have, that a number of basic pagan beliefs are alien to your general society. In some cases they may even be illegal.

Although religious tolerance is deemed to be part of modern Christian belief, it appears that extending that tolerance to the pagan belief system and its rituals is a little more than Christian society can cope with. So be prepared for some difficulties.

Welsh paganism and Druidism were both well-established and potent entities well before Christianity arrived in any of the Celtic nations. There are numerous publications, written by a range of extremely learned authors, that discuss this issue in much more detail than is necessary here. It is useful, however, to recognize that most historians would support evidence to suggest that the Christian church, in order to make its doctrine more easily accepted and understood, superimposed many of its beliefs and ritual celebrations onto existing pagan beliefs and rights.

One example of that is the Celtic cross, which literally superimposes the Christian cross emblem over the pagan symbol for the sun god, the circle. It has been suggested that because the circle is always shown as significantly smaller than the cross, and because the cross always appears in front, or "on top of" the circle

The Celtic cross is a clear illustration of the domination of the early pagan religion by the new Christian church. The circle, representing the pagan sun sign, is dominated by the Christian cross. This combined imagery also demonstrates that the Christian church retained much of the pagan imagery and tradition in order to ease the introduction of its new doctrine.

when represented in three-dimensional form, that the amalgamated symbol is a religious/political emblem showing the dominance of Christianity over paganism.

Many other examples can be seen if we consider the dates of Western Christian holy days. Most are undeniably superimposed on the far older pagan celebrations.

Needless to say, at a time when religion and politics, church and government, were literally one and the same, the law supported the church, and the church, for the most part, determined the law. Why then should we be surprised to have inherited a legal system that supports Christian belief and a Christian moral code to the exclusion of all others?

Some areas of ritual and practice described in this book will prove to be totally acceptable in modern society. Some others, with a little thought and consideration, will also work out fine. Still others, however, will be deemed unacceptable and illegal if exercised in public.

Remember that what we are trying to do here is reconcile pagan practices and a Christian moral mind-set and Christian law, bearing in mind that neither can be compromised and still be meaningful.

There are three areas where I have experienced major difficulties:

- Public nudity, particularly of aroused males, and the performance of sex magic rituals involving physical contact in public.

- Same-sex practices; paganism, in this tradition, recognizes no difference between homosexual and heterosexual relationships, but some rituals and practices conducted in the gay/lesbian version would be considered illegal in some societies.

- Anal stimulation and penetration, which could be interpreted as an illegal, obscene act in some societies.

There is not, and has never been, any doubt that any involvement of children, animals, and non-consenting individuals is totally unacceptable and rightfully illegal in all societies and religious cultures, including paganism.

THE JOURNEY

BEGINS

The Pen-Rhiw Chapel (1777 c.e.) originally at Dre-fach, Felindre, Carmarthenshire, South Wales. Now re-erected at the Museum of Welsh Life, St. Fagans, Wales.

Every individual choosing to involve him- or herself in a pagan ritual or practice has a fundamental, personal obligation to research and understand the law in regards to that particular practice. In some countries the law restricts a small number of the activities involved in Celtic sex magic to being practiced in private, between consenting adults.

It is the responsibility of the practicing Druid priest or priestess to ensure that all the rituals he or she conducts are not offensive to those involved. Fortunately, pagan rituals do not allow for spectators, so all those present at any ritual will be active participants and will be there by personal choice. In these circumstances it is unlikely that anyone will take offense at what ensues, but the priest or priestess must ensure that everyone is fully aware of what is to unfold before any ritual begins.

As everyone present will be a participant and play some role in the ritual, there is clearly a need for some form of instruction and organization of those involved. Each ritual described in this book is accompanied by precise instructions for the organization and conducting of the rite or practice. Through the application of common sense and consideration to others they may be expanded or contracted to suit the number of people involved without compromising their validity.

The Role of Emotion
in a Sex Magic Ritual

This is one of the more difficult and dangerous areas for any ritual or practice that involves physical contact, sexual activity, and intercourse.

Difficulties inevitably arise when people in a committed relationship become involved in activities with other individuals without the consent or knowledge of their partners.

For some couples, the involvement of one of the partners with the full consent of the other appears to cause no problems. For others, the idea is inconceivable.

In other cases both partners become happily involved with the group's activities. Some couples become involved but limit their contact to each other, while sharing the common activities of the ritual with the group.

It is not for me or anyone to dictate or judge other people's behavior. The pagan belief system offers an individual space for involvement in both a committed relationship and the group sexual activities involved in Celtic sex magic rituals. An individual's decision whether or not to become involved should be based on the belief system and moral code he or she embraces. The one and only precondition is that the decision be an informed one, based on adequate knowledge and an honest belief in what he or she is committing to.

In the case of couples considering becoming involved in Celtic sex magic with a group or in the privacy of their own relationship, it is essential that both individuals are equally committed and that both have an adequate understanding of what is involved.

From my experience with a wide range of groups, I can say that involvement based on lack of knowledge and understanding of what is involved—deception by one or other of the partners, impulsive decisions, lack of honesty, unfair persuasion, coercion, sexual gratification or other forms of superficial deliberation—only and always result in disaster. Such behavior can result in broken relationships, dissolved marriages, hatred, vindictiveness, and the abandonment and dissolution of the groups involved.

Detailed research, an in-depth knowledge of the subject, and an honest belief in what you are becoming involved with are the cardinal prerequisites for a rewarding experience with Celtic sex magic.

One topic, more than any other, is repeatedly brought up and questioned, most often by women: "What about love? What role does it play in sex magic? What effect does participating in sex magic rituals have on an existing loving relationship?"

The answer is twofold.

First, a shared emotion of love between the participants involved in a sex magic ritual is not necessary. Some people would even argue that it is a hindrance.

This is not to say that sex magic rituals cannot be performed between loving couples. In fact, some couples become involved with rituals only between themselves, in the privacy of their own homes.

General research suggests that it is easier for men than for women to participate in the sex act without the emotion of love being involved. Some women may oppose that suggestion vehemently. Whatever the case, the point is that some people feel that a loving relationship is essential before lovemaking can take place. This is an eminently honorable attitude and should be respected as such. It is extremely unlikely that people holding this view would ever wish to become involved in sex magic rituals involving anyone outside their own relationship. There should then be no difficulty in respecting their private relationship and values by leaving them to their own devices.

Problems sometimes arise, however, when people with a love-before-sex mindset attempt to impose their moral values upon those who do not share their views. The answer is found in the acceptance of freedom of choice for the

individual. Providing each person is furnished with all the information necessary to make a truly informed decision, the choice belongs to the individual, and to the individual alone.

It is important to be aware that the purpose of sex magic ritual is not to form loving bonds and relationships. These have no role whatsoever in the ritual or its intended outcome, which is simply to project the strongest possible energy generated through the most powerful orgasm that can be achieved. This is how we energize our spells and influences to maximum effect. The emotion of love is not an essential element of this pursuit. It is predominantly a sensual and spiritual experience that energizes our workings.

The second aspect of the question of love is that if the involvement of a member of a loving couple is undertaken in a deceitful or dishonest way, it can in fact extinguish any love that previously existed and ruin what may have been a caring and rewarding relationship.

In general terms, it should be the earnest intention of all those involved in sex magic practices to avoid emotional involvement. Affection will lead to jealousy, love will lead to possessiveness, relationships will lead to isolation.

Inevitably, all groups have their own dynamic. For better or worse, human nature will surface and produce circumstances that challenge and threaten your group. How you deal with these matters will be a measure of your own skill and maturity.

THE ROLE OF
EMOTION IN
A SEX MAGIC
RITUAL

Health and Hygiene

Throughout history Welsh Druids and Druidesses have played a major role in the health and well-being of their communities. One of the more well-known Welsh Druids of the late nineteenth century, Dr. William Price, not only introduced the forerunner of the British National Health System, but also legalized the process of cremation in Great Britain. Dr. Price, in addition to being a self-professed Arch Druid, was a medical doctor and the youngest person to have graduated from the Royal College of Surgeons in London. He lived a fascinating life in and around the small Welsh village of Llantrisant, some two miles from my hometown.

Recognizing that people were in a much better position to pay for medicines and medical treatment when they were in good health, able to work and earn money, Dr. Price introduced a system in which individuals made a small financial contribution to a personal fund each week while they were in good health. This fund then paid for any medical costs when they became ill.

It was many years later that a Welsh politician championed in the British Parliament a very similar idea, which in turn burgeoned into the British National Health System.

Herbal remedies and preventive medicine play a large role in Druidism, and many Druidic rituals are concerned with inducing good health and banishing harmful influences. These trends have greatly contributed to the fastidious cleansing and hygiene elements that precede each rite.

Some of these cleansing rituals are purely symbolic; others employ age-old traditional herbal sterilizing agents; still others invoke primal earth energies for purification and cleansing. There are two fundamental purposes for the cleansing and purification elements that precede each ritual:

- The purification of the inner spirit, the mind, and the body's energies. This preparation includes the clearing of any mental impurities, preoccupations, and prejudices in order to develop a focused, open-minded, clear mental state. The participant must be able to focus, because this is a major element of all Celtic sex magic activities, and he or she must be open-minded in order to conquer social prejudices and embrace the pagan/Druidic belief system. A clear mental state is essential if the participant is to fully appreciate the subsequent ritual and project all of the body's energy as required.

- The cleansing of the physical body. Whether the participant is involved in a solo or group ritual, physical cleanliness at the outset and continued hygienic practices are essential.

Although in the past little was understood about the transmission of disease and infection through unhygienic practices, there has still been a long Druidic tradition of bodily purification using herbs and other cleansing preparations. Only in recent times has science identified many of these potions as being effective sterilizing and cleansing agents. Alternative and complementary health-care practitioners now employ a number of these herbs and potions, while others are the subjects of mainstream medical research.

Although much is being discovered in support of these traditional techniques, we must acknowledge that there is insufficient evidence to support using these traditional practices to the exclusion of more modern, proven methods of hygiene. In the true Druidic tradition, we shall assimilate the new into the old and use all of the traditional techniques supported by modern hygiene practices that have proven scientific validity.

Because Celtic sex magic rituals can involve intimate physical contact, the potential for sexually transmitted diseases is inevitably present. The following checklist of guidelines has proven to be valuable to the groups that I have been involved with.

- General "safe sex" techniques should be rigorously adhered to.

- Condoms are recommended for all rituals and practices that involve physical contact of genitalia and/or male ejaculation. It will become

obvious as we progress through this book that it is the energy, not the product, of orgasm that is important to our magic. The sperm produced is, in all but one ritual, irrelevant (inconvenient, even messy). Female orgasm does not necessarily involve the same difficulties.

- Do not conduct or participate in any rituals if you have any unhealed or open wounds, cuts, sores, shaving cuts, abrasions, or other skin ailments.

- Thoroughly sterilize every ritual tool, fetish, phallus, and other implements before use. If they are to come into contact with any sensitive areas or are to be inserted internally, they must be covered with a condom or other effective sanitary protection. Do not exchange or reuse any ritual tools without replacing the condom or sterile covering.

- Blood is a potential carrier of serious infection. At all costs, avoid creating even the smallest skin lesion. These can easily result from overly rough bodily contact, attempting to insert large objects into small orifices, and so on. Some of these eventualities can be avoided by using lubrication aids and the like. We shall look at these in detail later.

- When forming a new pagan group, all participants must agree to undergo certified medical examinations and screening for transmittable diseases. Pool your medical certificates and agree to repeat the process every six months or so. If new initiates join your group, be sure that they provide the same certified medical evidence.

- If you or any member of your group experiences any illness, irritation, or discomfort or suspect any infection, consult your doctor immediately. Make sure all the other members of the group are informed immediately so that they may react accordingly.

- If you have a medical condition (such as a heart complaint, asthma, or high blood pressure), limit your involvement to what you (and your doctor) consider to be safe practices.

- If prior to, during, or following your involvement in any ritual you experience any ill effects, cease your involvement immediately and seek medical advice.

THE JOURNEY

BEGINS

22

- Be alert to whether others in your group are experiencing any medical difficulties leading up to, during, or following the ritual. Be prepared to act should you observe someone showing signs of illness or stress-related symptoms.

- Ensure that one or more of your group's members is a trained first-aid practitioner and that he or she is present before every ritual begins. Some of my groups arrange for a small financial contribution at each meeting in order to fund first-aid training costs for at least two of their members.

By applying these strict, simple, and effective hygiene practices in your group and as an individual practitioner, you can avoid most difficulties. Remember that the time to make these rules and the arrangements to carry them out is before any ritual or practice begins. Once you become immersed in ritual, you will be absorbed by other preoccupations; make sure that plans for safe practices are in place so that they become a routine and integral part of your activities.

HEALTH AND

HYGIENE

The Three Fundamentals of Celtic Sex Magic

eeply embedded in the practice of Celtic sex magic are the same three basic concepts that inform Druidism as a whole. In English they may be translated as the Three Fundamentals. It is these Three Fundamentals that separate Celtic sex magic from sexual exploitation, undisciplined sexual gratification, and other forms of magic that use sexual techniques.

It is essential that anyone practicing Celtic sex magic fully understand the Three Fundamentals, for to understand the Three Fundamentals is to understand the basic essence of Druidism and Celtic sex magic.

The words in bold lettering in the descriptions that follow are the ones for which I have had to choose the most appropriate, though not always wholly accurate, English translation. The concepts involved are complex enough without the additional confusion of unfamiliar Welsh words and phrases. The translations are clumsy and, I think, inadequate, but they are accurate within the limitations of the English language.

The Prime Fundamental

The pursuit of the true understanding of the Prime Fundamental has been the basic preoccupation of most Druidic practitioners throughout history.

To some extent the Prime Fundamental eludes accurate definition. In Welsh it is best described by words that have no precise English translation combined with melodic tonal expression on the part of the speaker that gives subtext to the literal meaning of the words.

Put simply, in the most appropriate words I can find, the Prime Fundamental is the basis of the Druidic belief system that I grew up with. It goes something like this:

The **cosmos** is made up of **essential energy.** Everything in the **cosmos** is made up of, contains, and is **powered** by this **essential cosmic energy.** It cannot be **created** or **destroyed.** It can, however, be **relocated,** and when a human being, animal, plant, or any other living organism ceases to exist in its bodily form, its **essential cosmic energy** is returned to the **collective energy.**

When a new physical form is created, it draws its **essential energy** from the **collective energy** of the **cosmos,** thereby perpetuating the **eternal energy cycle.**

Cosmic energy is present in all aspects of nature in differing forms. For example, it is this **cosmic energy** in various herbs that gives them the beneficial or harmful effects that we experience. In a scientific context, this **cosmic energy,** working in one of its forms as photosynthesis, **powers** the growth of these herbs and drives the formation of the chemical content that scientists are now beginning to identify and understand. As of yet, they have found no way of analyzing the other **powers** and **energies** contained within the herb that reach beyond pure chemical content.

Cosmic energy is also present in what could be described as the nonliving elements of nature: wind, **gravitational forces, magnetic forces,** fire, water, earth, the other planets of the universe, time, and so on. Literally everything is in the **cosmos.**

I have attempted to explain the Prime Fundamental in as simple a form as possible, focusing mainly on its relevance to Celtic sex magic. As you might imagine, the philosophical model of the Prime Fundamental is immensely complex and sophisticated when applied to all aspects of the Druidic belief system, but for now, the explanation above is adequate for our purpose.

The Secondary Fundamental

Because everything is **powered** by the **cosmic energy** of the **eternal energy cycle,** we can affect the events of the present and future by influencing and channeling this **cosmic energy,** whether in an isolated individual or in the form of the **collective energy.** This is achieved through the power of **generated influential energy** and the **guided channeling** of **inherent energies** (such as those present in herbs, water, and so on) produced through Druidic rituals and practices.

The Tertiary Fundamental

The concentrated and explosive energy of sexual orgasm is a powerful vehicle for projecting this **generated influential energy** into the **collective energy** for the prime objective of **effecting change** for the good of individuals or society as a whole.

In a contemporary interpretation, if we accept the scientific principle that every action produces an equal and opposite reaction, then we should also be able to accept the idea that the huge release of energy we experience during sexual orgasm must result in the production of an equally powerful influence.

The Three Fundamentals in the Sex Magic Ritual

The purpose of Celtic sex magic is to use the intense explosive power of the sexual orgasm as a vehicle to launch our **spell** or **influence** (our **generated influential energy**) into the **collective energy** in order to:

- Effect a change in the **collective energy** resulting in a positive, beneficial reaction.

- Direct this **generated energy,** via the **collective energy,** toward an individual or group for their benefit and well-being.

We intend to employ the **guided channeling** of **inherent energies** for the same purpose.

The Preparation of the Spell or Incantation

There are two stages in preparing the spell or incantation that you want to project. These are:

- Identifying the spell or influence that you wish to be wrapped in and transported by your generated energy, and defining it in an accurate incantation.

- Identifying where you want to project this generated energy, that is, its destination or receptor(s).

Both items must be identified prior to the ritual, usually at a special meeting of the participants who will be involved.

The purpose of the spell and where it is to be directed can be derived from any number of sources. Maybe a member of your group will have a particular concern he or she wishes to be addressed. Perhaps you will have reached a time of the year when a particular thanksgiving incantation may be appropriate, or perhaps you or a member of your group is embarking on a venture or journey that you would wish to support or energize.

Whatever the reason for the ritual, it is essential that you prepare your incantation in advance of the ritual.

We have all heard the fairy stories in which wishes are misinterpreted and chaos ensues. It appears that most leprechauns, genies, and fairies derive their entertainment from granting unsuspecting heroes three wishes and then misconstruing them for their eternal amusement.

I am not suggesting that you will end up in a genie's lamp if you get this wrong, but it is important to make sure that your incantation is accurate and expresses your wishes in as simple a form as possible.

I have never been an advocate of expressing spells and incantations in archaic language. I avoid all those thees and thous as much as doth seem possible. Good, plain, simple language is easier for everyone to understand and avoids any possible misunderstandings that may result from using obscure words and expressions. Remember, every participant in a group ritual must fully understand the content and meaning of any spells or influence involved so that each can add his or her energy to its projection. Stick to a vocabulary that everyone can understand.

Having defined your spell or influence, write it down, copy it, and circulate it to the other group members so that they can critique it and suggest alterations if necessary. During most rituals the participants will be required to chant this spell repeatedly; it is to everyone's benefit if they fully understand it, and it is even better if everyone can memorize it.

Well-crafted spells and incantations achieve the best results. However, spell crafting is a skilled art, and like all arts it needs practice and refinement. Take to heart the maxim: "Be careful what you wish for, as your wish may come true."

Confine each ritual to the projection of only one spell. As an individual or group orgasm is required to project each spell or influence in its generated energy form, it may be overly optimistic to expect to be able to project more than one spell in any one ritual. Most, if not all, rituals are prepared on this basis.

Once you have accurately defined your spell or influence, you are ready to identify the destination or recipient(s) and how your incantation will arrive at its particular destination. There is no point in spending time and energy defining a precisely worded spell of influence if you then send it into an eternal void. The process of directing your projected generated energy begins with the development of a visualization.

Writing the spell or intention down helps to clarify its meaning and ensure its understanding, and it also produces a written script for the whole Gathering to follow.

Visualization

Our intention is to develop a visualization of the journey that our generated energy will undertake as we project it through the collective energy of the cosmos to its destination. Everyone's visualization will be different, but all can serve the same purpose.

To visualize the entire cosmos filled with a collective energy, and a stream of generated energy traveling through it to a specific destination, is a gift given to few. Even after years of practice these things don't come easily.

The best method for learning is to take it step by step. The Druidess who taught me the majority of the ideas, practices, and rituals I have included in this book introduced me to this concept.

Practice the visualization before the ritual begins so that you have a clear and vivid image to project the generated energy to.

A Simple, Tranquil Meditation Technique

Meditation, even in its most simplistic form, is a complex and profound discipline far beyond the immediate purview of this book. However, we must arrive at a practical technique of meditation in order to allow us to explore and develop our visualization of the collective energy.

The one I was taught as a child is similar to a relaxation technique I was introduced to in Sweden, and one that I had, without instruction, explored and used to try and send myself to sleep when I was too excited to relax. The technique involves relaxing each part of your body in turn, starting with your toes, then each foot, then each leg below the knee, and so on, until only your mind remains

One of my favorite meditation spots, on the shore of Lough Leane, Killarney (the "Lake of Learning" in English), with Innisfallen Island in the distance. Innisfallen Island is famous for being one of the major ancient seats of Celtic learning and the place where the "Annals of Innisfallen" were created. The Annals were written by the monks of Innisfallen and remain as one of the oldest remaining accounts of ancient Celtic life. The island and the abbey ruins are still accessible by rowboat and are a focal point of ancient energy, creativity, and arcane Celtic power.

active. Thinking back to these occasions now, I can scarcely remember getting very far. It has always been a very effective sleep relaxation method for me.

The Druidic technique, however, requires a little more concentration, as we intend to arrive at a state of tranquillity rather than sleep.

The first step is to place yourself in a relaxed, tranquil environment where you are unlikely to be interrupted. You may best be able to relax in a quiet room in your home, for example. Burn your favorite incense, dim the lights, light a few candles, use a little essential oil in an oil evaporator or as an anointment on your neck and shoulders—whatever you find most helpful for relaxing. Alternatively, a favorite outdoor location may be equally suitable. Only you will know exactly the environment you need to find in order to achieve a relaxed, creative state of mind.

Having found or constructed your meditation setting, make yourself part of it by sitting upright in an erect but comfortable position.

Begin by seeking a general state of relaxation. First relax the shoulders, rotating them very slightly in order to make yourself more conscious of them. Feel yourself gently pushing down the extremities of your shoulders. This in turn makes you aware of the tension in your neck. Rotate your head slightly and feel the muscles in your neck relax.

Having relaxed your neck and shoulders, become conscious of your breathing. By progressively controlling your breathing, seek a slow, deep breathing pattern. Filling your lungs with each breath, make yourself aware that you are using parts of your lungs that you rarely employ. Maintain this controlled breathing awareness until you achieve a regular enhanced breathing rhythm. This part of the premeditation preparation is particularly elating when carried out in the open air. The feeling of filling the entirety of your lungs with pure, clean air and the effect of the increased oxygen intake can be extremely exhilarating.

Once settled into the enhanced breathing rhythm, begin to focus on each part of your body in turn, starting with the toes.

Wiggle the toes slightly to make yourself more conscious of them. Then feel a warm, relaxing glow flow over them.

Move on to the feet, focusing on each one in turn and relaxing them in the same fashion.

Continue to progress through each part of your body until your whole body is wrapped in a relaxing glow.

Don't rush through this process; let your body relax in its own time. Only when you are entirely relaxed should you begin to focus on the subject of your meditation.

For some people, achieving this relaxed state creates a sense of floating or

Meditation is an essential element in most Druidic practices. Simple tranquil meditation provides the platform for the development of all of your visualized journeys and environments.

detachment from the everyday world. This can be the starting point of a spiritual journey or out-of-body adventure. The main problem most people experience at this point is that they relax to such a degree that they fall asleep.

It is only by remaining constantly aware of the purpose of the exercise—arriving at a state of peaceful tranquillity of mind and body in order to meditate upon the details of our visualization—that we can focus on the development of our creation.

Beginning the Ritual Visualization

Begin by visualizing the recipient(s) of your spell or influence in surroundings that would be familiar to them. Picture him or her at home, in a favorite chair, standing in the kitchen, at his or her desk at work—anywhere he or she is likely to be when the spell is projected. Make sure that this is a strong image. Concentrate upon it; fix it vividly in your mind. Look around the scene and visualize the details—the furniture, the colors, the textures, how the location is lit. Every small detail helps to fix the visualization in your memory.

Then focus on the recipient. Develop a detailed visualization of the person(s) concerned. Begin with the face, the hair, the eyes, and so on. As you start to pull away from the person, continue to develop the picture by adding the details of clothing, including colors, textures, fabrics, jewelry, and any other details that come to mind.

You now have a detailed visualization of your recipient placed within familiar, equally detailed surroundings.

Continue to draw away from your recipient, developing your visualization of the journey as you get further and further away from him or her. Traveling away from where you've pictured the recipient, for example, you may pass through a door, into a second room, through another door to a hallway, out through yet another door into the garden, down the path to the gate. . . .

Every now and then stop and add more detail. If you are outside, visualize the garden or the outside of the house, once again adding colors, textures, flowers, grass, trees. Take the time to look around and take in as much as possible.

By now you will have realized that what you are doing is traveling the journey of the projected generated energy carrying your spell in reverse. By doing this, slowly moving away from your recipient and his or her surroundings, you are preparing the route for your return journey. After you have projected your generated energy using the force of orgasm, you will visualize its journey along the path you are now creating, stopping where you have stopped in this practice visualization and absorbing the same details on your return.

Choose a point on your reverse journey where it becomes difficult to absorb the growing amount of detail in the ever-widening scene. At this point allow your image to blur.

This is the point where you enter the collective energy.

Now is the time to review your visualization. Is it embedded firmly in your mind? Can you make the same journey again, recalling all the details you have added? Can you, in fact, make the journey in reverse, as you will need to do in order to project your spell during your ritual?

Many people choose to practice this part of the visualization journey over and over again until they have fully absorbed all the detail. Some add more detail on each journey. Whatever your choice, be sure that you have a detailed visualization of this part of your journey before you progress further. Your visualization should begin with the face of your recipient and conclude with a blurred image that marks your arrival at the edge of the collective energy.

If this is your first visualization of a generated energy projection, you are now entering a new and strange environment. If you have made this journey many times, you will already have a detailed visualization of the collective energy.

The Collective Energy

Every spell, influence, and meditation we enact is directed to or through the collective energy. So you should spend some time gaining an understanding of what "collective energy" means before you start trying to visualize it.

Once you achieve your initial visualization of collective energy, you will return to it time and time again, adding to it, developing it, and continually building the detail, making the end result uniquely yours.

This very detailed and personalized visualization is essential for connecting your personal internal energy seamlessly to the collective energy. In the case of sex magic your personal internal energy is concentrated and channeled through your orgasm. It leaves your body as generated energy, carrying your spell or influence on its journey through the collective energy to the intended recipient.

The realm of collective energy has been variously described as the other world, an alternative dimension, the fairy realm, a parallel universe, the underworld, Heaven, Hell, and many other equally intriguing names. It is a world where supernatural entities may coexist with humans, without our usually being aware of them, a world where spirits, fairies, guardians, and other beings dwell.

For us, it is a realm of pure energy. It is the original source of our personal internal energy, the origin of what may be called our soul. It is also the place to where our personal internal energy will return once our physical body fails. There, it will become part of the collective energy until once again it enters a living form.

The spirits, fairies, guardians, and otherworldly images some of us see and communicate with are manifestations of this collective energy projected into our perception. Whether they actually temporarily "exist" in our earthly world or whether they are channeled through our personal internal energy and we "project" them onto our world as recognizable images is, when all is said and done, immaterial. In both cases their origin is the collective energy.

Describing this collective energy has challenged people's imaginations since the beginning of time. Most historical descriptions reflect the influences and fashions of the time of their origin. The vivid world of green pastures, woodland, lakes, and mountains under a crystal clear blue sky, as described to me by my grandfather, was very convincing to me as a young boy. Although I always understood it to be another world, I gained comfort and a deeper understanding from this idyllic version of a world much akin to the one I saw every day. It was easy for me to accept its existence and value its importance.

Today, this simplistic visualization seems naive. We now think we understand much more about energy and nature. We are exposed to scientific information and images that influence our imagination. Similarly, science fiction has taken these images and developed them into fantastic projections of energy in space and environments far beyond our forefathers' imagination.

All these images and impressions will have at least some effect on how you visualize the collective energy. Whether you choose to develop a natural visualization, reflecting the energy and forms found in nature, or choose a more "scientific" imagery, embracing modern ideas of pure energy, it is imperative that you understand that it is the same collective energy that is being visualized in both cases. There is, without doubt, an infinite range of potential visualizations that can be drawn from an infinite range of source imagery. But it is always the same collective energy that is represented.

Although each person's visualization of the collective energy is unique to him or her, there are a number of features that their visualization must have in common.

There must always be an entry/exit point into the collective energy at the near side or beginning of the journey. This portal serves as the entry point into the collective energy on our outward journey and an exit point from the collective energy on our return journey.

There must also always be another portal into the collective energy at the far side or end of our journey. This portal represents the exit point from the collective energy on our outward journey and is also used as the entry point into the collective energy on our return journey.

Depending on the individual's choice, portals may be a simple doorway, a gate, a clear patch in a misty landscape, or a castle gateway. While any image can represent a portal, the image should be compatible with the rest of the visualization. Most importantly, it must represent a definite passing from one environment to another.

Not every projection of generated energy finishes its journey with a specific recipient. Some are directed toward the collective energy itself. These projections carry spells and influences generated with the intention of attracting energy or benefits from the collective energy, or otherwise affecting the collective energy and its related forces in some way. This type of projection does not require you to journey through the collective energy and out the other side but, instead, to enter the collective energy, implant the spell or influence, and return the way you came.

So, in addition to entry/exit portals, you need somewhere within the collective

energy a place where you can implant generated energy, a spell, or an influence.

My grandfather described an image of a spectacular bush at the center of the sylvan visualization he created for me. This bush represented the pure heart and energy source, the very core, of the collective energy. I developed my own visualization of the journey into the collective energy and to this bush. Parting its leaves and branches, I saw a core of pure white energy, into which I projected the generated energy and spell. I fed my influence into the life energy of all creation and returned to my known world with a feeling of immense achievement and a profound belief in the effectiveness of my journey.

I made that journey many times in my youth. Each time I nurtured and guided the progress of my generated energy and its related spell to the heart of the collective energy, projecting it into the core and returning with a sense of electrifying well-being.

As an adult, I created a more sophisticated visualization, one that I constantly use and develop to this day. But I often contemplate that original, naive visualization and the simple, uncomplicated thrill I experienced on my journeys into and through my personal verdant utopia.

Now you have created a visualization of the collective energy with two entry/exit portals, one on the near side, the other on the far side. These portals or thresholds afford access into and out of the collective energy. You have also visualized a core energy point within the collective energy where you can "deposit" your projected generated energy in order for it to merge with and influence the collective energy in a profound way.

By doing this you have created a visualization through which you can project and transport your spell or influence from its generation source to its recipient. You can then use this visualization to project to other individuals and groups and to influence the collective energy.

There is, however, one other major source of energy that you need to be able to access and influence.

THE JOURNEY
BEGINS

Latent Energy

By now you know that collective energy is present in all things, at all times, and that it cannot be created or destroyed. Its presence is patently obvious in active, mobile life forms, but it is not so obvious in inanimate objects. In the case of these inanimate objects ("inanimate" is a poor translation from the Welsh expression), the energy is usually dormant in the form of latent energy.

Although latent energy is dormant, it can be aroused and activated in order to influence the world around it or to affect the personal energy of those close to it. To accomplish this, you must be able to project the generated energy carrying your spell or influence directly into the inanimate object whose latent energy you wish to use. You can do this in one of two ways.

First, use a visualization of the collective energy to form a bridge or thoroughfare from the point of projection to the recipient, in this case the inanimate object.

Second, place a visualization of the inanimate object within the existing visualization of the collective energy and project the spell directly to its internal latent energy, reviving it and channeling its influence to your purpose.

You need a specific place, therefore, within the visualization where you can locate these visualizations of inanimate objects when you wish to include them in your workings. This location must be a firm, stable element within the visualization, capable of sustaining the object you place there.

So, in summary, you now have all the basic elements needed within the visualization: entry/exit portals, a core energy point, and a stable location for the visualization of inanimate objects.

But this leaves you with a very bare, uninspired visualization. Now the real work of adding infinite details to the visualization begins. You will want to create special places for yourself, places to go to experience particular emotions, places where you can retreat to in order to refresh your spirit and gain inspiration, places where you can seek solitude and solace. You will have a place for every occasion and need.

All this is a lifetime's work. But for our immediate purpose you need a

passageway through the visualization, a route for your projected generated energy. So, for now, we will return to our main objective.

A Brief Review of the Journey

To recap, we are defining the visualized passage of generated energy, the carrier of your spell or influence, from its point of projection to its recipient.

You began by visualizing your journey in reverse, starting at a powerful visualization of the recipient in a familiar environment and progressively moving backward, away from the recipient, until you reach a point where your visualization becomes a blur.

Through this blur you now visualize the far-side entry portal into the visualization of the collective energy.

You enter the collective energy and travel through it via your now familiar path toward the exit portal on the near side. For now, you stop at the threshold of the exit portal, seeing before you the same blurry, misty vista you saw at the far-side portal.

We now need to fill in the final detail: the journey from the exit portal to the very point of projection of the generated energy.

Generated Energy: The Point of Projection

Reading about it, this may seem to be the simplest part of the visualization. It's not so easy during the ritual, however, as this is the part of the journey you will be taking immediately following your orgasm, when you will have to apply the whole of your powers of concentration and focus.

The point of projection is the point of focus from where you project your spell or influence as generated energy. The point of projection for men is the precise point in the scrotum where the major power of contraction occurs during the initial force of ejaculation. For women this point of projection is in a similar location but deeper within the body.

Some people, however, see the point of projection within the brain, most often at the base of the back of the brain. They suggest that the energy begins there, travels down the spine to the sex organs, and is projected from their body via their orgasm.

You may adopt either of these philosophies. You may even, as many people do, find your own point of focus within your body as your own point of projection. The choice is up to you. What's important is that you find the point within your own body where your orgasm originates. This is the point from where the power of your generated energy derives. Everyone's will be different, but each is profoundly important.

From the point of projection, generated energy travels with the initial force of your orgasm to the point of exit from your body, where its external journey begins. The point of exit from the body for men is obviously the tip of the penis, and the time of exit is the moment the first ejaculation leaves the body. For women, the point of exit is the opening of the vagina, and the time of exit is the exact moment the feeling of the first contraction of orgasm begins.

Our purpose now is to trace the journey of generated energy from the exit portal of the collective energy back to the body.

We left our journey standing on the threshold of the exit portal at the near side of the collective energy. Through the blurry mist we begin to form a visualization of the landscape containing the building or location where our ritual is taking place.

Moving closer, fill in the detail of the landscape around the location of the ritual. Move closer still, visualizing the exterior of the location and moving toward an entry point to gain access.

Passing through the entry point, travel through the building (if appropriate) to the room where the ritual is taking place. Observe the surroundings and fill in details as you progress.

Once in the room, halt to fill in details such as decor, colors, furniture, and so on.

Finally, move toward a visualization of yourself, in the position from which you are to project the generated energy.

Getting closer, observe the details of your own body. Move to your body's point of exit and then through it, ultimately arriving at the point of power from where your projection originates.

The Complete Journey

You have now completed the entire journey, in reverse, through three environments: the near side, where your projection begins; the collective energy; and the far side, where your recipient resides.

As you made the journey you created detailed visualizations of each of the environments and your progress through them.

Each time you make this journey, or each time you make journeys to other recipients, you will add more detail to your visualization. Throughout your life you will continue to refine your visualization, creating more and more exit/entry portals, each giving access to different destinations. You will add more and more special places within the collective energy where you can visit to fulfill your needs and desires. It will become a place where you explore your real self.

You will power your journeys by visualizing your generated energy traveling through these now familiar territories. This will be your process of spell projection and spell binding.

Tools for the
Working of Celtic
Sex Magic Rituals

The popular image of an ancient Druid usually portrays an aging, white-bearded man in long, flowing white robes, with a crop of mistletoe in one hand and a golden sickle in the other.

Both mistletoe and the sickle have significance in the Druidic tradition, but it is also true to say that the Druidic tradition employs many other herbs, barks, flowers, and minerals in its workings and uses a broad range of tools in order to craft its rituals, spell castings, and remedies.

Unfortunately, the golden sickle has never been one of these tools. We have seen that the role of the true Welsh Druid/Druidess was in providing a service to the community in which he or she lived. He or she was, and still is, usually born and bred within that same community.

A Druid's status in the community was reasonable high, but when you consider that the majority of these communities were agrarian, existing on a purely subsistence level, it is not too difficult to understand that few, if any, Druids would have possessed a golden sickle.

Another, purely practical problem related to the golden sickle myth is one you will easily understand if you have ever tried to harvest mistletoe. Mistletoe is a hardy, tough plant. It clings tenaciously to its host and needs a very sturdy, sharp blade to cut and separate it from its growing place. Gold, by its very nature, is not up to this task. Even if a Druid or Druidess were fortunate enough to be bestowed with a golden sickle by a wealthy patron, it would prove to be a useless tool for everyday use.

There is, of course, the cardinal rule that mistletoe must not be cut with an iron knife. This practice is shared by all Druidic traditions (i.e. the Welsh, Scottish, Irish, French, etc.). It is also shared by many pagan belief systems that consider mistletoe as a sacred plant. Gold, however, is not a practical alternative. Bronze was the chosen alternative for most ancient Druids/Druidesses, and it was possibly mistaken for gold by ancient Roman historians. Nowadays, as most blades are made from steel, the choice of a suitable metal no longer causes a problem.

Putting this and other romantic notions of magical golden tools aside, let's take a little time to list and describe the usual collection of tools and accessories that a practicing Druid/Druidess will need to have at hand, noting, in particular, the range of tools and vessels used to craft the Celtic sex magic rituals detailed later in this book.

Attire

The process of preparing your body and mind prior to your ritual is described in detail later, but in simple terms it involves shedding the clothing and mental state of your everyday existence, cleansing your mind and body, then casting a circle and assembling the setting for your ritual.

Participants in Celtic sex magic rituals are always naked. Apart from the fact that the naked body provides direct contact with the elements and nature, most rituals result in direct sexual contact of some form or another.

However, once the body has been cleansed it is usual to wear some form of loose-fitting robe while continuing the preparation for the ritual. Some Druids/Druidesses wear robes created especially for this purpose; others, like myself, adapt more commonplace garments for the occasion. I currently use a traditional Moroccan jalaba; some of my colleagues wear Indian caftans, while others have made similar loose-fitting, long robes for themselves.

The main thing to bear in mind is that the garment has to be loose fitting in order to allow freedom of movement while you are arranging the setting for your ritual. It will also have to be relatively easy to remove prior to beginning the ritual.

Colors are important, more so to some people than others. We all recognize that colors can influence our moods and attitudes, and we should bear this in mind when choosing the color of our garment.

Whenever possible Celtic sex magic rituals should be worked outdoors, which allows direct contact with nature and the elements. This, of course, has some bearing on what we wear.

Cleansing usually takes place at home. If the ritual is to take place in your garden or near your home, it is relatively easy to slip on a tunic or ritual robe after cleansing and then arrange your setting. If the weather is warm and dry, it makes this task even simpler.

But if you are traveling some distance to a favorite grove, riverbank, or other secluded setting for your ritual, you may want to give your clothing a little more thought. There is nothing more stimulating than participating in sex magic in the open air, naked, on a crisp winter's day, or feeling the rain on your naked body while you are deeply engrossed in your ritual. But arranging your setting and casting your circle on a cold, wet day in nothing but a flimsy robe can be a disaster.

Be sensible about this aspect. Don't worry about having to wear some form of traditional garb to do all your preparation. The ancient Druids wore long robes and the like simply because it was the dress of the day. It is far more important that you be warm, dry, and in a positive state of mind when you begin your ritual than that you be dressed in a fancy but impractical robe.

Other aspects I have been asked about on a number of occasions are the matters of body hair, body piercing, and tattoos. I raise them here, as they do not readily fit anywhere else in the text.

In some traditions both men and women shave their bodies completely before each ritual. In fact, in France I was told of a ritual designed specifically for this purpose; it preceded a fertility ritual based on pagan practice.

Other schools of thought suggest that the body should remain entirely unshaven. This could be a little impractical, especially for females living in today's fashionable world.

All the groups I currently work with have adopted the practice of clean-shaving

TOOLS
FOR THE
WORKING
OF CELTIC
SEX MAGIC
RITUALS

the whole of their bodies, with the exception of the hair on the head and facial hair for men. The feedback I receive suggests to me that people like the hygiene factor and also find the shaven body more sensual in both men and women.

The choice belongs to you and your partner or group. I have no reason to believe that either option is more effective than the other insofar as the ritual is concerned.

Body piercing, body ornamentation, and tattoos have a long tradition in Druidic history. Making the body as attractive as possible can only enhance your sex magic activities. Whatever you, your partner, or your group find attractive and stimulating is the thing you should do. Whatever you choose to do, do it with commitment and enthusiasm.

As far as other body adornments are concerned, simple headbands can look attractive and prove useful for those with long hair. Both men and women may wear neck chokers and other forms of jewelry. Other items such as decorative waist chains, ankle chains, belts, armbands, and the like are often seen worn at pagan gatherings.

The Wand

The wand is the most important tool for any Druidic priest or priestess. This is the instrument used to connect to and channel energy. The wand directs your personal internal energy, connects you to the collective energy, and allows you to channel and redirect latent energy.

I crafted my first and most simple wand with the help of my grandfather. I still have it in my collection. It was cut from a rowan tree growing at the center of our local forest, crafted in the shed in my grandfather's garden, and energized in a ritual at the side of our local river.

All Druid priests and priestesses own and use a collection of different wands, each with an individual power and purpose. I now have a collection of about fifty wands, each of which has unique features and is energized for different applications. Fifty, I admit, may be a little excessive, but one of the major interests and talents of my family heritage is the crafting and energizing of Druidic wands. So naturally, in addition to giving many wands to other Druid practitioners, I manage to hold on to most of my favorites.

Wand making is a complex and detailed skill requiring understanding of the natural forces and energies involved, some basic craft skills, and immense patience. A number of years of my Druidic training were dedicated to this tradition.

The most important features in achieving the utmost control and power generation from a wand are the wood(s) from which it is made, the process of its manufacture, and the energizing rituals that empower it. However, I would need an entire book and more to begin to explain the detail and skills necessary for the art of crafting and energizing wands. As you will need a wand for your own workings, I will focus on some of the main elements involved so that you may craft or acquire a simple but effective wand of your own.

Harvesting and Crafting a Simple Druidic Wand

The starting point is finding the donor, the tree from which your wand will be given to you.

Returning momentarily to the Three Fundamentals, we remember that collective energy is present in all things, and that it lies dormant as latent energy in inanimate objects. So whether we perceive a tree as an inanimate or animate object, we must acknowledge that it has, in some form or another, its share of the collective energy. It is this energy, in part, that we intend to capture in the small part of the tree that will become our wand.

Each individual species of tree has its own characteristic energy from which we may benefit. These varying characteristics allow us to use and channel the specific energies related to each tree.

The most appropriate time to harvest your wand is when these energies are at their strongest. For the most powerful wands, this time is spring, when the tree's energy is at its most active, flowing into the outer regions of its branches and feeding rapid growth. For more subtle wands, used in love working and other gentle workings, the best time to harvest your wand is in autumn, when the tree's energy is concentrated, flowing back into the tree's core.

Every tree's energy is influenced by the other energies surrounding it. These

TOOLS
FOR THE
WORKING
OF CELTIC
SEX MAGIC
RITUALS

influencing energies may be drawn from the interaction of all the living things within the vicinity of the donor tree: from the trees adjacent to it who may well share the same root complex, from the grass and ground plants covering the surface of the earth in which it is growing, from mosses and lichens that may be living on the tree, or from other plants growing in symbiosis with the tree, such as ivy, climbing holly, and so on.

One of the manifestations of collective energy in our world is what has come to be known as magnetic force. This, in its most obvious form, is an easily witnessed phenomenon. With compass in hand you can "see" magnetic force in action for yourself.

Magnetic force, which flows from the south toward the north, has a strong effect on a tree's energy, channeling it most powerfully to the north side of the tree. It is from this north side of the tree, then, that we want to harvest our wand.

We can, given the time, work with our chosen tree and nurture a specific branch for harvesting. This must be done with care and respect for the tree and in a kind and gentle manner. Gentle binding may accurately align chosen branches with the northern cardinal point, in order to maximize their potency. Lesser twigs and small branches may be carefully pruned from the chosen branch to strengthen it. By these methods of minimal intervention and nurturing, your chosen branch will flourish and, when harvested, make a splendid wand.

Another factor that some people consider influential to the potency of a wand is the time of day (or night) when the wand branch is harvested. I myself was taught that the precise time of day or night that the wand branch is harvested is irrelevant, with one important caveat: Wands harvested in the daytime belong to the realm of the sun and therefore have a male affinity. These wands should be used only by male Druid priests. Wands harvested during the nighttime, particularly those harvested under bright moonlight, belong to the realm of the moon. These therefore have a female affinity and should be used only by female Druid priestesses.

Now you are ready to harvest and craft a wand. For simplicity's sake, I advise you to choose either a rowan (mountain ash) tree or an oak tree. Both species contain the properties you will need for sex magic rituals.

Every tree's energy is enhanced by the other energies surrounding it. Here the energy of a sturdy oak is enhanced by the attributes of the holly and ivy growing upon it.

TOOLS
FOR THE
WORKING
OF CELTIC
SEX MAGIC
RITUALS

49

In early spring, during the day or the night depending on the gender of the user, select a straight-ish branch of about thirty inches in length from the north side of the tree. Don't be tempted to harvest the first suitable branch you see; wait until you feel a strong affinity with the branch you are contemplating harvesting. You will, believe it or not, know the right branch when you see it.

Harvest the branch about one inch from the trunk of the tree. Once you've made the cut, seal the stub left on the tree trunk with wax or another suitable sealant. Do the same to the cut end of your wand.

There is a specific ritual for this harvesting process (see part 3), but it is not essential in this case. This is to be your first functional wand, used only for your Celtic sex magic rituals. The harvesting of your next wand can be more sophisticated. You can explore the wand harvesting ritual then.

You now have your basic wand branch. Before you take it home, remove its leaves and lesser twigs. Cast them at the base of the donor tree in order to return their energy to its source.

You will now need to store your wand branch for around three weeks. Lay the branch with its tip facing north and its cut end facing south. In this way the earth's magnetic force will continue to enhance the wand's energy.

After three weeks carefully remove the bark from the wand. Keep the bark, as we will need this for the cleansing and energizing ritual. Replace the wand in its north/south orientation for another two weeks.

After this final seasoning, trim the branch using a sharp knife to produce a smooth-surfaced wand. You may, if you wish, then seal and polish the wand using natural beeswax.

For the purpose of sex magic rituals you will need a wand that is feathered, that is, a wand with its last inch or so beaten to produce a brushlike effect. To achieve this, place the far end of the wand (not the end you will hold) on a hard surface. With a small hammer, gently beat the last inch of the wand as you rotate it, until it begins to feather. Do not be tempted to beat it hard to speed up the process; this will cause the tip of the wand to break off.

Keep gently beating and rotating the wand tip until the feathering becomes brushlike, with the "brush hairs" becoming quite fine. Occasionally roll the wand

tip between your fingers and thumb to help to separate the fibers of the wood and assist in developing a smooth feathering effect.

Once the desired feathering is achieved, bind the tip of the wand just below the base of the feathering with cotton or another natural fiber. This prevents the brush fibers from "splitting" along the length of the wand.

Lightly brush the tip of the wand across the palm of your hand to help separate the "bristles." You can also gently roll the tip between fingers and thumb.

A traditional technique at this point is to wash the wand tip and then gently chew it. Your saliva and the gentle chewing movement of your molars further refine the wand feathering. The choice here is entirely yours. I do use this method with no problem or side effects, but I can well imagine that some people might not be too excited by the idea. To do this, however, you must be knowledgeable about the tree from which you take your wand branch. Do not partake of this tradition unless you have a thorough knowledge of the properties of the tree you are using. Some woods and barks are poisonous, and chewing them will produce ill effects and even, in extreme cases, death. Certainly do not chew a wand made from the wood of a yew tree, as it is definitely poisonous. Never do this with a "found" branch, no matter how sure you think you are of its species.

When the feathered tip is perfected to your liking, trim the end of the wand into a rounded, brushlike shape using a sharp scissors.

You have now created your first wand, and the time will soon come to cleanse and energize it. Until then continue, as always, to store your wand in the north/ south orientation.

There is a school of thought that suggests that wands should be gleaned or collected from the forest floor, having been dropped there as a gift from the donor tree. Conservationists may well support this theory, and I can understand why. Druids are by definition also conservationists, but this idea contradicts everything I was taught about wand harvesting and crafting.

It is fundamental to the effective use and power of each individual wand that the wand crafter and the Druidic priest or priestess using the wand know the precise tree from which it originated, where on the tree it grew, and when it was

TOOLS
FOR THE
WORKING
OF CELTIC
SEX MAGIC
RITUALS

harvested. Each of these factors influences the unique qualities of a wand and its suitability to its user, as does the method of handling the wand branch immediately after its harvesting.

In my opinion, none of these factors can be accurately defined for a "found" branch. How then can it be crafted into a functioning wand? Without knowing all of the aspects that may have had an influence on the tree and therefore the wand, it is not possible to know the wand's attributes and therefore use it to best effect. The only way of doing this is to actually harvest the wand yourself or receive it from someone who will guarantee its provenance.

As we shall see later, there is a harvesting ritual that, if adhered to, will ensure that we receive the best possible wand without offending any of nature's laws.

Wand branches may be harvested from any sort of tree. Each tree, however, has its own characteristics. Centuries of experience and spell crafting have given us information on how these characteristics may be channeled for different purposes, making some wands more suitable for certain rituals and workings than others.

The basic idea is to match the intrinsic characteristics of the wood to its use. In this way you have the most powerful influences working on your behalf.

Below I have listed the more common trees found in the natural environment where Celtic sex magic first evolved. Each one is listed with its associated characteristic.

Tree	Associated Characteristics
Apple	Fertility workings and by association good health and long life. Also associated with love workings.
Ash	Healing workings and those workings used for strengthening spells and influences. A very powerful wood to use in projecting and channeling energies.
Beech	Workings used to expand knowledge and guide learning.

Birch   Cleansing workings. One of the trees associated with lunar influences.

Cherry   New relationships. Used extensively in initiation rites.

Elder   Associated by the Celts with moon workings. Always used by Druidesses and female Celtic priestesses. The tree with the most powerful female influence. Also a fairy tree, with a wealth of associated magical properties.

Elm   Love workings. Also workings to induce rest, relaxation, and sleep.

Hawthorn   Purification and cleansing workings. Male sexuality and potency. Used extensively in Celtic sex magic.

Hazel   Another tree used in fertility and potency workings.

Holly   Protection, especially protection against negativity. Used in the absence of the dagger to seal the protective Circle.

Ivy   Used as a wand, but more often wrapped around a wand of other wood to strengthen "binding" workings.

Mistletoe The plant traditionally associated with Druidism. History suggests Druids knew this plant as "the all-healing plant." For us, the most powerful channeler of fertility and sexual potency.

Oak   The most sacred tree of the Druid tradition. The supreme tree of male power and potency. One of the most used woods for sex magic wands. Unfortunately, very difficult to craft.

Pear   Workings related to female fertility and sexuality.

Rowan   Also called mountain ash. Mainly associated with the lunar/female influences of the Celtic tradition. Frequently used for wands for sex magic rituals.

Sycamore   Used to strengthen projections and influences.

Willow   The Celtic moon tree. Associated with lunar/female influences. Used by Druidesses and priestesses conducting sex magic in order to

TOOLS
FOR THE
WORKING
OF CELTIC
SEX MAGIC
RITUALS

strengthen their female influences. Favored in lesbian sex magic for its channeling of female power.

Yew　　　　Used mainly for casting/projecting and binding long-term spells and influences. A very popular wood, used extensively for wands by the ancient Druids.

This list represents only a small selection of the trees that yield suitable woods for wand crafting. These are the trees whose characteristics and associations most influence sex magic.

You will also have noticed that some of the above are not really trees. Mistletoe and holly are both parasitic creepers that grow on host trees. However, they are very potent plants in their own right. Most often, their influence and potency are added to the characteristic associations of the wand by wrapping a length of the chosen plant around the shaft of the wand or stave prior to performing the ritual.

Similarly, some wands are actually crafted from more than one wood. Compound wands, as they are called (or at least that's the best English translation), are made up of two or sometimes three woods twisted or plaited together soon after harvesting, when the wand branch is still "green" and supple. These compound wands take on the combined characteristics of the woods they are made up of. By carefully selecting the woods involved, you can craft compound wands with a wider and more concentrated power than those crafted from a single wood.

You can also craft wands for very specific purposes. Consider the influences you most want to affect your spell. Carefully select the most appropriate and powerful woods for your purpose. Plan the nurturing, harvesting, crafting, and energizing of your wand to complement the working of your intended ritual. Having carefully constructed your wand from the chosen combination of woods, bind them together to combine their influences. You may then choose to wrap it with mistletoe or holly or both to increase its influence even further.

These "specifically crafted" wands, when used for the purpose for which they were made, are the most powerful tool at a Druid priest/priestess's disposal.

A two-piece compound wand, showing how two branches, harvested from trees with compatible attributes, may be woven together to form one wand. This effectively combines the complementary attributes of both woods in a synergy of power and energy focused upon the purpose of the ritual for which it is to be used.

The Staff or Stave

The staff or stave is another very important Druidic tool featured in many representations of ancient Druids. It functions as the symbol of the Druidic priest or priestess's authority as the facilitator of the ritual.

Unlike the case of the wand, each Druid priest or priestess has only one staff or stave, which is usually kept and used for his or her entire life.

The staff or stave is a very personal object of power used for connecting to, channeling, and generating energy. It is used to draw or "cast" the Circle, the enclosure within which rituals are worked. It is also used in rituals by the leading priest or priestess for a variety of functions.

TOOLS
FOR THE
WORKING
OF CELTIC
SEX MAGIC
RITUALS

As a potential initiate, a young person harvests his or her own stave in much the same manner as a wand. The staff becomes a regular companion for the young person as he or she progresses through the early stages of the tradition. It accompanies the young person wherever possible. I even took my stave to school with me, which worked well because my school was at the edge of a large forest, quite a walk from home. My stave was accepted by my school friends as a whimsical walking aid and, along with my slight build, contributed to my schoolboy nickname of "Stick."

Ideally a stave is crafted from oak. It is normally about 6 inches taller than its owner. It is a substantial branch, requiring much longer seasoning than the wand (around three months), after which it is fashioned, sealed, and polished with beeswax. It is then cleansed and energized in the same way as the wand.

Your stave will grow in power as it matures. You will find it an invaluable asset, friend, and comforter as well as an awesome tool for your workings.

The Dagger

The dagger appears in some form or another in most ancient religious rites, as well as modern Wiccan and natural magic practices. It is unnecessary to cite its significance in other practices; suffice to say that in the context of Celtic sex magic it plays a powerful role.

Physically, the dagger must be double-edged, black-handled, and contained within a scabbard. Like all the other objects used in Druidic rituals, the dagger has to be cleansed and purified and then empowered or energized. See part 3 for more information on these rituals.

The dagger will probably be the most contentious tool you use. Often associated with satanic rites and ritual sacrifice, the dagger appears in nearly all the negative images of Druidism, witchcraft, and the occult. When was the last time you saw a horror movie without the mandatory sacrificial knife being included?

The dagger's role in the Druidic tradition is far from the misconceived bloodletting sacrificial weapon.

In other forms of sex magic the dagger represents the male form, the penis or phallus. In Druidism it is mainly a symbolic weapon of defense, used at the begin-

One of the ritual daggers I use in my work. The dagger plays a major role in all Druidic rituals and, unlike the ubiquitous Druidic sword and golden sickle, it was one of the earliest ritual tools used by the ancient Druids.

ning of every ritual to seal the protective circle within which the ritual is worked. The dagger is drawn three times and then left partly drawn at the entrance to the Circle as a warning to unsympathetic and contrary forces. This ancient element of Druidic rites can still be seen in the public Chairing of the Bard ceremony at the Welsh National Eisteddfod.

As this dagger is never ever used for cutting or piercing, for safety's sake it is best kept blunt. Contrary to popular belief, we are not going to be offering live sacrifices or mutilating bodies in worship of Satan. We will leave that to the imagination of less enlightened individuals.

The dagger can be a simple, functional instrument or, as some practitioners prefer, an overly decorated status symbol. I have seen vastly expensive antique weapons used for this purpose; to me this seems to change its significance, making it an object of desire rather than a symbol of protection. But to each his own.

Keep in mind that knives of all kinds, including ritual daggers, may be defined as offensive weapons in some localities. Check out the laws relating to knives in your community and be sure to abide by them.

My first dagger was a simple affair, a Boy Scout's sheath knife with a wooden handle that I stained black and a brown leather sheath. It served the dual purpose

TOOLS
FOR THE
WORKING
OF CELTIC
SEX MAGIC
RITUALS

of ritual dagger and the sharp knife I used for harvesting and crafting wands.

Like a small number of my present-day ritual tools, the dagger I now use was a gift. It was made by a Bedouin tribesman of the African Sahara, and it was given to me by a friend while I was on a tour of northern Africa.

On the subject of gifts, there is a school of thought among Wiccan and other similar practitioners that all meaningful tools should be received as gifts and not harvested, crafted, or purchased by the person who intends to use them. I know individuals who subscribe to this school of thought and have benefited from it. The power they generate from their workings is significant, but I have yet to be convinced that it is borne out of this philosophy.

My own teachings lead me to believe that all your Druidic tools and equipment will grow in power as you do, maturing and becoming an extension of your own being. I have already mentioned that I was taught that knowing the origin and history of your tools is essential, and that harvesting and crafting some of the more important items is the only way to achieve the desired results. Therefore I cannot subscribe to the "gift" principle, but I fully understand the belief and commitment of those who do. I am happy to have as gifts my dagger and a few other items that I do not have the skill or means to manufacture myself. I believe that they carry with them the positive energies and attributes endowed upon them by the friends who gave them to me.

The Chalice

The chalice is another functional object with huge ritual significance. Like the dagger, the chalice can be a simple, purely functional object or a decorative symbol of status. What's important is that it be waterproof and clean, as it is intended to contain liquids, some of which we will be consuming as libations. The chalice cannot be made from metal or have any metal decorations that are likely to come into contact with its contents; glass or ceramic is the favored choice of material. The chalice must be able to be sterilized.

The vessel must have a diameter of at least ten inches at its top. This is to allow easy access to the surface of the liquid it contains.

The chalice represents the female form and the female sex organ.

A libation vessel filled with metheglin, a libation goblet, a wooden ladle, a copper ladle, and heating candles sometimes used to heat the libation in the copper ladle.

Libation Vessels

In some rituals the chalice holds a libation used during the rite. Rather than pass the chalice around as a communal drinking vessel, I always choose to use smaller drinking vessels to distribute the libation among the gathered group. Ordinary drinking glasses are more than adequate for this purpose. Alternatively, ceramic or pottery goblets are also suitable. Again, they must be easily sterilized and cannot be made of or decorated with any metal.

Ensure that there are sufficient libation vessels available for the number of participants involved in the ritual. In my experience, an average glass or goblet will hold enough of the libation for three participants.

TOOLS
FOR THE
WORKING
OF CELTIC
SEX MAGIC
RITUALS

The Ladle

A ladle is needed to transfer the libation from the chalice to the drinking vessels. Again, it must not be made of metal. Wooden or ceramic ladles are readily available. You can also use a small ceramic or glass jug with a handle.

The Cauldron

In Welsh tradition, the cauldron is a large, black iron pot that serves as a cooking pot for the family's meals and is suspended by a handle over a fire.

In the context of Druidic ritual, the cauldron is a smaller metal vessel used to mix, burn, boil, and otherwise prepare the concoctions used by the priest or priestess. You will, for instance, be using a cauldron to burn the bark stripped from your newly made wand during its cleansing and energizing ritual.

Any suitably robust metal vessel may be used as a cauldron. Try to find one about eight inches in diameter.

The Phallus

The phallus is the first ritual object to be discussed that is used only in sex magic. Phallic objects are seen in a wide variety of religious contexts throughout the world, from China to India, Australia to North America. The ancient Egyptians, Romans, Incans, Mayans, and Greeks all used phallic objects in their religious rites.

In most European pagan belief systems, ritual daggers represent the male phallus. Uniquely, Celtic sex magic employs a specific phallic object to represent the male sex organ, its energy, and its power.

Along with the wand, which in some circumstances also represents the male sex organ, the phallus is used both to channel energy and to represent the penis in acts of simulated intercourse.

The phallus is usually crafted from wood and fashioned in the exact shape and to the exact size of the typical penis. Sometimes the phallus includes representations of testicles, and sometimes not.

Nowadays, many practitioners use commercially manufactured artificial penises. Readily available from sex shops and mail-order companies, made from a variety of materials, most commonly rubber and latex, they are anatomically correct reproductions of the male sex organ. These modern versions are designed to be used as penis substitutes and are therefore ideally suited for use during sex magic rituals.

Whatever you decide to use, bear in mind that the phallus will be repeatedly inserted into the vagina of the female(s) participating in the ritual. It must therefore be made of a hygienic material, easily sterilized, and easily covered with a condom.

In the case of female-only or lesbian rituals, specially designed strap-on versions of the phallus are also available. These may be used as appropriate throughout the sex magic rituals in addition to the hand-held versions.

The Binding Vessel

The binding vessel is another tool unique to sex magic rituals. The purpose of the binding vessel, as the name suggests, is to bind together the participants, by which we mean the committed members of your group, in a powerful, unbreakable bond, creating a synthesis of the internal energies of all those involved. On the basis that the whole is greater than the sum of its individual parts, this synthesis provides a powerful energy source for all your ritual workings, as well as binding your group together in a formal way.

The binding vessel is a sealed vessel containing samples of earth taken from sources held to be of profound influence by individual participants. These are combined to form an inseparable compound, just as the internal energies of the participants are bound together to create the powerful synthesis necessary for the rituals.

To create your group's binding vessel, each member initiated into your group must submit a small sample of earth, about an eggcup full, taken from a place with special meaning to him or her, whether the place closest to his or her heart or the place where the individual feels the strongest bond with nature and the elements.

TOOLS
FOR THE
WORKING
OF CELTIC
SEX MAGIC
RITUALS

These samples are mixed together and then ground in a mortar and pestle into an inseparable compound. This grinding process is done meticulously until all the components are ground into a very fine powder.

The compound is then refined with each of the other base elements—air, water, and fire—before being sealed into the binding vessel.

The details of this ritual are described later in this book.

The Working Stone

As you progress and develop your workings and rituals you will find you will need a dedicated surface upon which to work. This is the function of the working stone.

I have deliberately avoided calling the working stone an altar because that term carries connotations of acts of worship. We have seen that Druidic practice is not an act of worship. Contrary to some schools of thought and unlike some other pagan belief systems, there are no gods to be worshiped in Druidism. The essence of Druidism is the Three Fundamentals, as previously explained.

The working stone can be as simple or as elaborate as you like. I have never considered it to have any actual influence on the spells and rituals that are carried out on it. It does, however, need to be functional, and when the tools of the ritual are arranged properly upon the stone it does add a certain weight to the rituals being worked.

Working stones vary enormously in style. They need not even be made of stone; in fact, they rarely are. I have used large flat stones still in their natural location and similar stones permanently placed in dedicated ritual spaces. I have also conducted rituals on folding tables covered in simple linen cloths. The workings in all these cases were equally effective.

What I believe to be important is that the working stone be aligned to the cardinal points to maximize the natural energies of its location. It should provide a sturdy and stable work surface, and it should be large enough to hold all the objects, instruments, and tools for your ritual, which should be laid out correctly so that the ritual can be carried out smoothly and to best effect. The working stone also needs to offer sufficient space for you to conduct the necessary workings with ease.

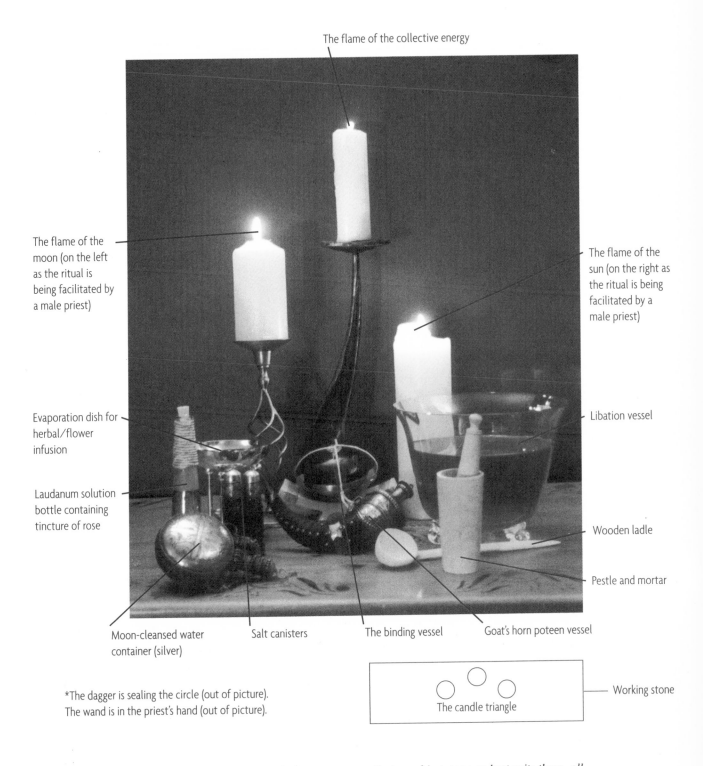

The flame of the collective energy

The flame of the
moon (on the left
as the ritual is
being facilitated by
a male priest)

The flame of the
sun (on the right as
the ritual is being
facilitated by a
male priest)

Evaporation dish for
herbal/flower
infusion

Libation vessel

Laudanum solution
bottle containing
tincture of rose

Wooden ladle

Pestle and mortar

Moon-cleansed water
container (silver)

Salt canisters

The binding vessel

Goat's horn poteen vessel

*The dagger is sealing the circle (out of picture).
The wand is in the priest's hand (out of picture).

Working stone

The candle triangle

*While it is up to the individual priest or priestess to arrange their working stone as best suits them, all
the essential ritual tools must always be present. Many priests or priestesses view the arrangement of the
working stone as a very creative and personal process.*

I also believe that if a working stone is made from natural materials, it inevitably harmonizes with the ritual better than one made from man-made materials.

The working stone and its covering cloth(s) offer an ideal opportunity for individuals to express their artistic talents. I have seen many wonderfully decorated working stone covers, each a unique work of art.

Different covers may be used for different rituals and workings. Each can be decorated to reflect the energies, associations, and influences of the particular ritual that it is designed to be used for.

It was important for me, as it may be for you, to bring together the environment of my working stone quite early on in my training. I found it gave me a sense of belonging and strengthened my commitment to my training. Having

This convocation stone is at the center of an ancient stone circle near Kenmare, County Kerry, Ireland. It is one of the very few that still remain aligned in their original location within the circle, and from my own observations, it appears to still be used quite frequently by a range of practitioners.

somewhere to go for the sole purpose of focusing on my Druidic experiences was important to me, as was the feeling of involvement and immersion in my workings that the environment of the working stone gave me.

The fact is that my first working stone, grand as the name may make it sound, was actually a board spread across two small bedside tables in an old stone outbuilding in our garden. All the same, it was a very important place for me, and it was there that I developed and nurtured the energies within me.

This simple working stone, adorned with very basic equipment—candles and candleholders, cover cloths, incense burners, essential oil evaporators, and so on—was more than adequate for my needs, and it served me well for quite a few years. I mention this simply to demonstrate that beginning your path in the Druidic tradition does not necessarily mean a large investment of money, scouring through antique stores for ancient ritual paraphernalia, or investing in equipment and robes from specialty stores or mail-order companies. Your involvement can begin, as did mine, with a simple walk in the woods to harvest your wand.

The Convocation Stone

Just like the working stone, the convocation stone need not be a stone at all. Again, in truth, it rarely is.

The purpose of this stone is to support the person who is to be the central focus of the ritual. Sometimes the convocation stone is a permanent, solid structure. Other times it is a trestle-style table consisting of two portable A-frames with sturdy boards laid across them.

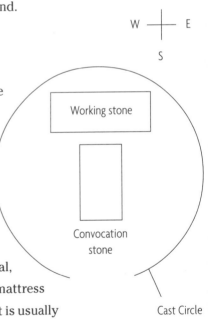

The convocation stone must be strong enough to support the weight of a full-grown adult. It must also be sturdy and rigid enough to allow this person to maneuver onto it, move around during the ritual, and alight from it when his or her role is complete. It may have a thin mattress and head pillow set on it, for the comfort of the participant. Likewise, it is usually covered with the same sort of decorative covering cloth as is the working stone.

The convocation stone is set up prior to the beginning of the ritual. It is placed within the cast Circle, between the priest or priestess and the working stone, allowing the entire group to draw near it and witness the workings of the ritual.

Candles and Candleholders

At the center of the working stone there need to be three candles. Three is, and has always been, the most powerful of magical numbers.

A tall candleholder is required for the central candle. Two shorter candleholders may be used for the two outer candles. The three candles are laid out in a triangular form as shown on page 63. All the candles are of natural color.

The central candle flame represents the collective energy. It is unmarked, as there is no emblem devised to represent it. The other two candle flames represent the sun and moon's energies and influences. One candle is marked with a small golden circle; this is the one that represents the sun. The other is marked with a silver crescent; this one represents the moon.

If a female Druid priestess is facilitating the ritual, the moon candle is placed on the right-hand side and the sun candle on the left. If a male Druid priest is facilitating, then the sun candle is positioned to the right and the moon candle to the left.

There are two other candles required in all rituals. These are placed at each side of the entrance portal to the cast Circle. They may be placed on floor-standing candleholders or in smaller candleholders placed upon tables. These candles, or more precisely their flames, are used as cleansing flames for all who enter the Circle. It is directly between these two flames that you place your partly sheathed dagger to seal the Circle before beginning your ritual working.

The ancient Druids lit small fires on each side of the entrance to the Circle to produce their cleansing flames. When you conduct your ritual outdoors, you could use fires instead of candles, but be sure the fires remain small and under control at all times.

Incense and Essential Oil Burners

The burning of incense and essential oils is common to most religious ceremonies throughout the world. In recent years it has also been the basis of a number of therapeutic practices based upon its restorative properties. Aromatherapy, in particular, acknowledges the way in which fragrances and inhalations affect our moods, frame of mind, and well-being. Add to this the belief that burning or evaporation is a method of projecting the energy and characteristics of the substance being vaporized and you begin to understand the importance of burning incense and essential oils.

Different incenses, essential oils, herbs, barks, and other natural substances are burned and evaporated for a variety of objectives during rituals and workings. Incense and essential oil burners are used in most indoor Celtic sex magic rituals.

Two incense burners or essential oil burners are placed on the working stone and lit at the beginning of the ritual. Cleansing herbs, incense, and essential oils are burned to purify the atmosphere. Subsequently, others are burned to relax and then stimulate the participants in the workings.

You will also use your cauldron, which will contain burning charcoal, to burn

The burning of herbs and incense and the evaporation of essential oils and herb infusions, as we see here, not only creates a beneficial atmosphere for facilitating rituals, but also releases the attributes of the aromatic herbs, barks, and spices used. This ancient Druidic practice is much akin to today's aromatherapy procedures.

the herbs, barks, and other substances used during your workings. You will need a small, fireproof surface on your working stone onto which you can place your cauldron. If you are using your working stone for your private workings and preparations in addition to your rituals, you may choose to use a small, out-of-the-way area of the stone for the cauldron. Place a number of ceramic tiles or a small metallic grid on the working stone surface to protect it and make it fireproof.

White Cleansing Cloth(s)

Although they are not actually ritual objects, a number of white cleansing cloths will be needed for your rituals and workings.

White is the favored color for sex magic rituals because it demonstrates the cloth's cleanliness. Natural fabrics like cotton and linen are preferred.

The Sword

You will have noticed that there has been no mention so far of the ubiquitous Druidic sword. I don't use one. I must admit that I have a ceremonial sword, given to me by a well-wishing friend, but I never use it. I fail to see its importance or relevance in my personal understanding of contemporary Druidic culture.

Some use it to cast the Circle; I use my stave. It is a much more natural and meaningful object, harvested, crafted, and energized by me.

The sword is also sometimes used in the Circle sealing rite. I use my dagger, which I also use for a variety of other workings, for this purpose.

Some use the sword to "draw down" the natural energies of the universe. I use a wide range of other objects to channel and project the specific energies I work with.

The Druidic sword also plays a significant role in the ceremonies of the Bardic tradition. In my opinion this diminishes its significance in the serious workings and rituals as I was taught them. The Druidic sword, like the golden sickle and the white robes, was introduced as a romanticized image of the archetypal Druid, and like these other objects, it is a product of the fashions of the time of its introduction. It is seen by practicing Druids as a symbol of artificially created

Druidic culture, which diminishes the significance of the true tradition.

For the greater part the sword is employed by bards in cultural/artistic ceremonies and by the official of the sanitized bodies who operate under the umbrella of benevolent Druidic organization as a part of their ceremonial regalia.

I see no role for the Druidic sword in my workings. This is a personal opinion that I have also found to be expressed by a number of my colleagues. There is, however, no substantial reason, outside that of "image," not to employ the use of the sword. It is the choice of the individual practitioner.

The Druid's Cache: A Checklist of Equipment

Your Druidic tools, cloths, vessels, and accessories are referred to collectively as your cache. If you are new to the concepts of the Druidic tradition, I suggest that you build up your cache piece by piece as each item becomes necessary to your workings. Ideally, begin with a wand that you harvest by the method described earlier. Learn to cleanse and energize your wand as described in part 3. Then learn to use your wand, channeling its attributes and using it to focus your energy, before you think about acquiring your next tool.

To summarize, your cache will eventually include:

- Wand (one or more depending upon your purpose)

- Stave

- Dagger

- Chalice

- Libation vessel(s)

- Ladle

- Cauldron

- Phallus (one or more)

- Binding vessel

- Working stone

- Convocation stone

TOOLS
FOR THE
WORKING
OF CELTIC
SEX MAGIC
RITUALS

- Candles and candleholders

- Incense/essential oil burners

- Cleansing cloths

This list is not exhaustive, but it contains all the essential equipment you will need to begin your workings. Your wand(s), stave, and dagger will be at the heart of most of your rituals and workings and will become your most significant and valuable tools. They will accompany you on your journey into the tradition. As you progress they will mature and become more powerful, just as you will.

The remaining items in your cache are of secondary importance and may be changed and substituted when and as you see fit. Some people may, for instance, have entire working stone layouts that coordinate in some way and are regularly changed with the seasons, or with daytime or nighttime rituals, or if a male or female is facilitating the ritual. The variations are endless.

The items that are required only for sex magic rituals, such as the phallus and binding vessel, can be added to your cache once you are confident that your knowledge, attitude, and abilities are sufficiently developed and you are prepared to become involved in this area of the tradition.

Some Compounds, Potions, and Ingredients

While you are working on accumulating the essential equipment, you can also begin to bring together some of the compounds, potions, and other ingredients you will need for your workings.

Again I shall focus only on the items you will require for your immediate needs. As you progress and grow in your craft, you will gather around you all manner of compounds, potions, tinctures, and other commodities to use in your workings. For now we will begin with the basic essentials.

Moon-Cleansed Water

To maintain the purity and integrity of your rituals and workings, you will use only moon-cleansed water. You will, of course, have to undertake the cleansing of water yourself, moon-cleansed water being not yet available in supermarkets.

The purpose of this cleansing process is to allow the influences of moonlight to purify the water. Although we now understand that there is, in fact, no such thing as moonlight, that it is just the moon reflecting the light of the sun, we also understand that everything is influenced by the collective energy. Sunlight is an expression or manifestation of the collective energy. Moonlight is a reflected, filtered presentation of the same phenomenon. This reflection and filtering alters the light's influences and associated properties. This, in a very simplistic way, is why moonlight has an effect different from that of sunlight.

Other aspects that contribute to the unique influences of moonlight as compared to sunlight are the moon's gravitational pull (another manifestation of the collective energy, affecting tides, winds, and weather), the difference in heat emission, and the different radiant light spectrums.

The working for moon-cleansed water is described in part 3. Once your springwater is moon-cleansed, it can be stored in its blue glass bottle in a cool place for an indefinite period.

Salt

Next to moon-cleansed water, salt is the most often used commodity in your workings. Salt has been used all over the world as a symbolic and practical cleansing agent throughout history.

Ordinary, store-bought commercial salt will not do in this case. In Welsh Druidism, salt is always evaporated from seawater. Sea salt contains, in addition to the basic salt, minerals that fix additional influences and benefits in the compound.

Some Druidic practitioners, particularly those in northern France, have the benefit of natural salt flats where unlimited naturally evaporated salt can be had all year round. The rest of us must work to harvest the salt from the seawater.

The salt you produce will be for symbolic cleansing and external use, not for consumption, but it still must come from pure, unpolluted seawater. If you cannot vouch for the purity of the seawater you collect on your own, then get a good-quality genuine sea salt from your local health food store or herb shop.

Ideally, collect your seawater from a rock pool on a hot summer's day, as late in the day as possible, when the seawater will already have evaporated to some extent, concentrating the salt you are going the extract. Collect the water before the tide returns, as the incoming tide washing into the rock pool will dilute the sea salt solution.

Some purists insist on allowing the collected seawater to evaporate naturally in sunlight. The argument is that by using natural evaporation the water is returned directly into the rainwater cycle, an important feature as water is one of the four basic elements. The salt and other minerals are then left as a gift of nature.

I agree with this philosophy wholeheartedly, but since I live in a country with such a damp atmosphere, this is an extremely lengthy process. The practical answer to this problem is to speed up the evaporation by heating the collected seawater.

THE JOURNEY
BEGINS

To do this, pour a cup of seawater into your cauldron and place it over a low heat source. I use a gas camp stove for this. The water will slowly evaporate, leaving a thin film of sea salt on the base of the cauldron. Now pour in another cup of seawater (leaving the original sea salt deposit in the cauldron) and repeat the process.

After a few repetitions the sea salt residue will be thick enough to collect, grind in your pestle and mortar, and store. This still takes quite some time and needs almost continuous attention. It is a good process to have going in the background while you are getting on with other aspects of your preparation.

Metheglin

Metheglin is the first Welsh word in this book that I have failed to find suitable English translation for. Its modern form is derived from the older Welsh word *meadyglyn,* which translates best as "medical drink." However, metheglin is much more than that.

Metheglin is used as a general pick-me-up, in a range of rituals, and as a specific medication. It is fermented for specific ailments using infinite combinations of herbs, flowers, barks, and spices. It was once considered as an almost universal medicine. Every Druid and Druidess has his or her own collection of metheglin recipes.

The medical attributes of metheglin, including its use as an aphrodisiac, have now, for the greater part, given way to modern drugs of one kind or another.

The main ingredient for the base drink is honey, which is fermented and infused with the selected range of herbs and spices. Long before the introduction of grapes for wine and barley for beer, honey was diluted, fermented, and drunk at all celebrations, feasts, and festivals. Its maker, the bee, has always been thought of as a precious, almost sacred insect, and its products are regarded as highly beneficial to mankind. Ancient Druids were fervent beekeepers, as were the Christian monks who followed them. To many people the bee still is a very special insect, and those who keep them are rather fanatic in their enthusiasm.

There are two basic versions of metheglin. One is flavored with spices; it tends to be sweet and is drunk mainly for pleasure. The other is flavored with herbs and tends to be less palatable. There is an infinite number of variations

on these two basic versions, combining herbs, spices, and other beneficial ingredients to produce whatever effect you may desire.

There are as yet no commercial suppliers of the potion, so you will have to make your own metheglin. Below is a recipe for a classic version of metheglin used as the libation during all sex magic rituals. This version has aphrodisiac properties and acts as a sexual stimulant. More reliable modern ingredients have replaced some of the older ones. This does not affect the end result; it just makes the whole process a lot simpler and the outcome a lot more predictable.

Ingredients

1.8 kg (4 lb.) brown honey

3.5 liters (6 pints) warm water (moon-cleansed water is preferable)

1 large lemon

20 g (3/4 oz.) citric acid (available from most pharmacists or wine-making suppliers)

2.5 ml (1/2 teaspoon) each of ground ginger, mace, cinnamon, and cloves

Brewer's yeast (same as used for wine or beer making)

200 g (7oz.) demerara sugar (available from many natural food stores)

1 campden tablet (available from wine-making suppliers to aid fermentation)

1 g potassium sorbate (available in powder or tablet form from wine-making suppliers)

Method

To prepare the must, dissolve the honey in the warm water. Thinly pare and chop the lemon rind, then add it to the honey solution along with the citric acid and the spices.

Squeeze the juice from the lemon and strain it.

When the must is cool, stir in the lemon juice and the active yeast. Pour the solution into a sterilized jar; fit an airlock to the jar and leave to ferment in a warm place for seven days.

Remove the lemon parings and stir in the sugar. Replace the airlock and ferment until the yeast activity slows almost to a stop (or until the specific gravity reaches 1.020, if you are the scientific type).

It is important that the metheglin remain sweet, since it is not so pleasant

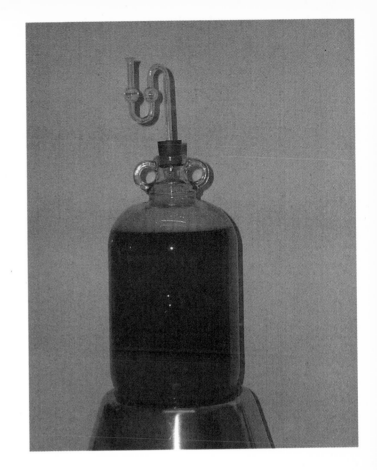

Metheglin fermenting in a demijohn with a modern airlock. The original practice was to place a wad of flax or clean cotton into the neck of the vessel in order to prevent the entry of unwanted airborne bacteria. The wad also restricted the amount of oxygen allowed to enter the vessel and thereby aided the final fermentation.

when all the sugar has fermented out. Although the metheglin is not at its best at this stage, the common practice to test its sweetness is to pour a little into a glass and taste it.

Do this before terminating the fermentation. If the metheglin is too sweet, allow the brew to continue fermenting until the desired sweetness is achieved.

Filter the metheglin into another sterilized jar, then add the campden tablet and potassium sorbate to terminate the fermentation.

Allow the metheglin to settle and clear in the jar, then siphon off into sterilized bottles.

Make sure the metheglin fermentation is terminated before bottling the brew, otherwise you can expect the storage bottles to explode as the fermentation continues.

Store for about nine to twelve months (depending on your patience) before consuming.

During sex magic rituals you can use your metheglin as a cold or warm libation.

To serve it warm, use the traditional mulled-wine method: Pour your metheglin

SOME
COMPOUNDS,
POTIONS, AND
INGREDIENTS

into your chalice, heat the tip of a medium-length poker or mulling iron until it is red hot, then plunge it into the metheglin.

Hold the poker or mulling iron with a cloth to prevent your hand from being burned, and stand back when you plunge it into the metheglin. Remember that you will be naked at the time.

This can be quite a spectacular way to provide your participants with a warm libation on cold winter nights.

Herb versions of metheglin are made in a similar way, but a faggot of herbs or bouquet garni is suspended on a thread in the fermenting must for one week or so until sufficient flavor has been extracted. The choice of herbs to use will become more apparent once you have studied their physical and magical properties. A very common household formula consists of equal amounts of fresh mint, rosemary, sorrel, and mace. This is a healthy pick-me-up and may be drunk at any time.

While the spice version of metheglin may be used as a warm or cold libation near the end of your sex magic ritual, another, stronger version may be used at the beginning of your ritual.

Ireland, Scotland, northern France, and Wales all have a version of locally distilled spirits. The most famous and well-known of these is the Irish poteen, which is distilled potato wine.

The poteen (or a local equivalent) may be added in a 50:50 ratio to the metheglin to produce a much more fortifying libation for the early part of your rituals.

A libation vessel containing a mixture of metheglin and poteen. In the forefront a mulling iron or heating poker, used to heat the libation. The iron is first heated in the fire and, while still red-hot, plunged into the liquid. Mulling the liquid in this fashion imparts a unique flavor to the libation and is the traditional way of heating winter drinks of all kinds in the Celtic Nations.

Poteen is the traditional Irish "moonshine." Almost every household has its own special recipe. It was (and still is) mainly produced by the distillation of fermented potato "wine" and can be extremely potent stuff. Other natural stimulants were also used by the Druids to increase consciousness, amplify creativity, and broaden the sexual experience. These include essences of "magic" type mushrooms, laudanum, root compounds, and some very dangerous, sometimes fatal concoctions from foxgloves and deadly nightshade. Shown here are a laudanum solution bottle, a goat's horn poteen flask, and a silver pipe for herbal mixtures.

77

PART 2:

How the Sex Magic
Ritual Works

This section of the book deals with what is undoubtedly the most difficult and controversial element of Celtic sex magic: the process of arousal and stimulation leading to sexual orgasm. We will also discuss the duality of the sex magic orgasm and how to harness the orgasm and the period of time immediately following the orgasm for your own use. We will look at how to maintain and augment the sensual force through sustained intensification, thereby promoting the most powerful and potent projection of your personal internal energy, which carries your spell.

My purpose in outlining the sex magic ritual in this part is to give you insight into the role that orgasm plays. The roles played by the priest or priestess, his or her assistants, and the participants are discussed in much greater detail in part 3. There you will find a step-by-step description of the invocations, responses, movements, and layout of each working and ritual.

I hope, however, that in addition to seeing the function of orgasm in the context of the overall ritual, you will develop a better understanding of the distinct responsibility the Druidic priest or priestess carries. As mentioned at the very beginning of this book, only the priest or priestess of the sex magic ritual is a Druid; the ritual requires no general membership in a Druidic clan. The participants in the rituals are celebrating a pagan rite, which acknowledges no gods or deities; it accepts only the sublime omnipresence of the collective energy.

By becoming involved in Celtic sex magic in the role of the Druidic priest or priestess, you are submitting to the Three Fundamental principles upon which Druidic belief system is based. But I am obliged to issue one strict warning: Celtic sex magic is but a small part of Druidic practice. If you intend to expand your involvement beyond this area, you must seek the additional knowledge that will make your efforts safe and rewarding. While it is true that there is nothing more hazardous than ignorance, it is also true that a little knowledge can be a very dangerous thing.

HOW THE SEX MAGIC RITUAL WORKS

Before we begin, we must take some time to consider the power of the forces we are going to become involved with.

The force of the sexual orgasm and its associated emotions have been responsible for the creation of empires and their fall; for wars and massacres; for great wealth and abject poverty; for the destruction of entire civilizations and for some of the world's most outrageous crimes. Sexual drive is unquestionably the most powerful force that mankind has some frail form of control over. Whether or not you choose to admit it, it is the most powerful driving force in your life. It is your most powerful desire; it is present in your conscious and unconscious selves more often than any other thought or motivator. It has changed and will change your life pattern in the most profound way. Without it, you simply would not be here.

You must be constantly aware of the immense power of the forces you will be channeling and using. Never underestimate the profound effect your sex magic will have upon you and the others you choose to involve in your practices. Remind yourself at every possible occasion that you are working with the most powerful force in the nature of mankind. Do not take this responsibility lightly; you are evoking the most potent forces in the cosmos.

HOW THE
SEX MAGIC
RITUAL
WORKS

A Preview of the Sex Magic Ritual

s it is for all natural events, the core of sex magic is a cycle, a series of events that you will attempt to anticipate and over which you will attempt to exercise a form of control.

Anyone who has experienced a sexual orgasm and the sensual stimulation preceding it will know that in order to exercise any form of control over the event one must be extremely strong-willed. You will be attempting to exercise a considerable amount of control over both your body and your mind during the whole process. This will be possible only with a thorough understanding of the cycle, knowledge of the techniques necessary for this control, and a considerable amount of training and practice.

The cycle of the sexual orgasm, from its build-up to the period following the orgasm, is woven into the core of the sex magic ritual. It becomes the Projection Cycle, the means and power of projecting your spell.

The Projection Cycle

The Projection Cycle is at the very heart of the sex magic ritual. It is irrevocably entwined with the natural cycle of the sexual orgasm. It begins with the first moment of sensual awareness; sometimes it even becomes the instigator of sexual awareness.

During this cycle your internal energy will leave what I can best call "the here and now" or "the conscious world" and undertake a visualized journey, returning only in the final moments of this part of the ritual.

The Projection Cycle is composed of seven successions. These are:

Awakening

Augmentation

Intensification

Quickening

Orgasm and Projection

Continuance

Relaxation

Each of these successions has significance in the ritual, as you shall see. Each has a definable threshold, a specific transition point when you pass from one succession to the next. The ritual helps you recognize these transition points by raising your awareness and heightening your senses.

From Start to Finish

Every ritual is worked within a protective Circle, so each begins with the creation or casting of this Circle. The Circle has an entrance portal, a simple gap in

Graphical Representation of the Seven Stages of the Projection Cycle

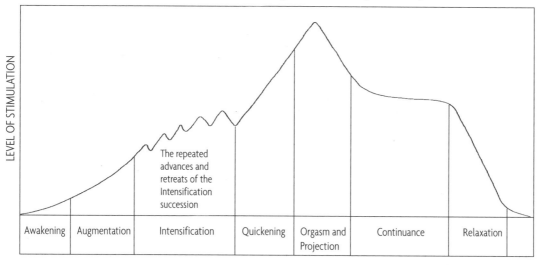

LEVEL OF STIMULATION

The repeated advances and retreats of the Intensification succession

| Awakening | Augmentation | Intensification | Quickening | Orgasm and Projection | Continuance | Relaxation |

the Circle through which all the participants in the ritual enter.

If the ritual involves more than one participant, the next step is the Gathering, when all the participants come together in the Circle and exchange brief informal welcomes.

The Circle is then sealed in preparation for the ritual. Cleansing and purification workings begin, and candles are lit.

Once the cleansing and purification workings are complete, the main ritual begins. A ritual libation is given and taken and the priest or priestess speaks the spell or incantation for the first time. The spell or incantation is then adopted by the Gathering; it becomes the focus and is chanted repeatedly by the participants.

The Principal Conduit is then named (we shall look at the significance of naming later), adopted by the Gathering, and anointed. The Principal Conduit is the man or, more typically, the woman upon whom the ritual is focused. The rest of the Gathering, including the priest or priestess, will focus their attention on this person, and he or she will govern the projection of the generated energy.

The second libation is given to the participants in the Gathering by the Principal Conduit.

The Principal Conduit then takes position on the convocation stone and the workings of the Projection Cycle are undertaken.

Once the Projection Cycle is complete and everyone in the Gathering has returned from their visualized journey, the Gathering reinforces the spell by group congress, that is, by the collective chanting of the spell, the singing of a prearranged song, or the chanting of a prearranged thanksgiving statement. The important factor is that this is a communal expression, demonstrating the like-mindedness and strength of the Gathering.

The final and main libation is then given and taken, the parting gift is given (this gift, as we shall see, is not a material one but a brief piece of wisdom given to the Gathering by the priest or priestess), and the candles are blown out in order to cast the Gathering's energy toward the collective energy.

HOW THE SEX MAGIC RITUAL WORKS

The Circle's portal is unsealed and opened, and the Gathering scatters. The Circle is then erased.

Now that you have seen how the Projection Cycle fits within the overall ritual, we shall look at each of the cycle's seven successions in detail.

The libation symbolizes the unity of the Gathering and underscores the principle of "giving and receiving," which is fundamental in all Druidic spell casting and spell binding.

Awakening

The Projection Cycle begins with the sensual Awakening, the raising of your awareness of your sexual senses and the initial arousal and stimulation of your sexual urges and organs.

Once the Circle has been sealed and the preliminary parts of the ritual are complete, we enter the part of the ritual that is focused on the spell, its reading, adoption, and chanting. When this is complete we suspend our focus on the spell and reorient the focus to the sexual Awakening.

Suspending Focus

Suspending your focus is a technique used repeatedly in sex magic rituals and workings. It involves placing the focus in the "back of the mind." You are not forgetting it but suspending it, putting it on temporary hold, storing it in your short-term memory for later retrieval.

The method I was taught for doing this is, once I have a very clear understanding of the spell or incantation being worked, to attach that spell to a visualization and make a conscious mental effort to place it safely in a place visualized in the mind.

I was taught a very effective visualization method in my Druidic training; it may help if you approach it in the same way. Visualize a strongbox or treasure chest located in a secure place in your memory. For this purpose your memory may be visualized as a place that is familiar to you in the conscious world, such as a secret chamber, a well-lit attractive cellar, a grove in the woods, or a secluded island beach. Picture whatever suits your personality. It needs to be a safe, well-loved place that you feel extremely comfortable in.

The Awakening, the first step in connecting with the collective energy and your individual sensual perceptions.

When you wish to suspend focus on a spell to concentrate on something else, define the spell clearly, visualize writing the spell on a piece of parchment, roll the parchment, make the visualized journey to your safe place, open your casket, and place the spell parchment inside. Close the casket and return to your conscious body to continue your workings.

When you need to retrieve your spell in order to continue working with it, simply make the visualized journey to collect it, read it from your parchment, and renew your focus on it.

You can use this technique whenever it is necessary to suspend your focus or concentration, including times when you are disturbed during your workings or when your meditations are interrupted.

Arousal and Stimulation

Having suspended our focus on the spell, we begin to focus on sexual arousal.

This is the point when we disrobe, revealing our true bodies and internal energy to nature and the collective energy. It is our first step in "connecting" with the collective energy.

The concept of naked rituals is, for some, difficult. The religious morals and social etiquette that many of us have been programmed with instill in us a suspicion or distaste for social nudity. Even though some of the more recent social philosophies suggest that nudity is a more natural and therefore more agreeable state, we are still circumscribed by our social prejudices.

Druidic tradition has always been, and still is, closely linked with naked ritual practices. I have never heard of or been involved in any sex magic rituals, workings, or practices that have been worked fully clothed.

Sex magic does, however, traditionally involve the decoration and adornment of the naked body in a way intended to stimulate the sexual senses, ranging from body piercings and tattoos to body painting and seductive clothing. Many female participants and priestesses adorn their naked bodies in a way that is deliberately intended to sexually stimulate and arouse the other members in the Gathering. This is not so often the case with male participants and Druidic priests. One reason for this phenomenon that has been suggested to me is that females do not experience the same amount of arousal from visual stimuli as males. My personal experience would reinforce this theory, but it contradicts what is usually the norm in nature, where most often it is the male of the species that is brightly and seductively decorated.

We have seen that the Druidic tradition makes no distinction between male and female or sexual orientation. Male Druid priests, however, have predominated throughout history. Although many women have become Druidesses and priestesses and have played a powerful role in Druidic tradition, it must be said that Druids have been, and still are, most often male. We shall see later, though, that females are almost always the Principal Conduit in the sex magic ritual, at least in heterosexual workings.

It is important that the priest or priestess facilitating the ritual have an intimate knowledge of each individual participating in the ritual, together with an understanding of the collective predilections of the Gathering as a whole.

One Gathering may prefer a predominantly "participative" style, in which case the priest or priestess must adopt a facilitative role. Another may be more oriented toward nature, in which case it is the role of the priest or priestess to facilitate the ritual in a way that reflects the overtly natural elements of Druidism.

A Wiccan witch, dressed in a collection of fetish accessories long since established as a representation of the dominatrix, facilitated a Wiccan ritual I once observed. Her adornment reflected perfectly the needs of the Gathering she facilitated. As a result of her adornments she appeared extremely dominant from the moment she entered the room and her appearance reinforced the very dominant style in which she facilitated the ritual. Her dominance interacted perfectly with the submissive nature of the members of her Gathering.

The ritual was immensely powerful and successful. Along with two other dominant priestesses, the Wiccan witch aroused the Gathering to tremendous heights of sexual energy. Knowing that the Gathering had a predilection for submissive behavior, the witches were able to dominate and control the Gathering's activities and sexual excitement to the point that the twenty or so participants all reached orgasm at the same moment. This produced an explosive projection of an intensity that I have rarely witnessed or equaled.

The point here is that all reasonable forms of sexual stimulation are suitable for ritual, and that if you have a good knowledge of the individuals in your group you will be able to adapt the role of priest or priestess in accordance with the predilections of the Gathering.

So the Awakening begins with the removal of outer clothes to reveal naked or adorned bodies to the collective energy and each other. It is usual at this point that a number of the Gathering will already be visibly aroused. This is, of course, more obvious in the male than the female. To identify female arousal is more difficult, but with practice and a certain amount of intuition you will soon become able to recognize the indicators: reddening of the complexion, erect nipples, widened pupils, changes in breathing patterns, and other bits of body language.

The remainder of the Gathering must also be stimulated into sexual awareness. This is done by the Communication, in which all the participants of the Gathering communicate verbally and physically with each other. They wander around the Circle meeting with each other, greeting each other and stroking each other's bodies. Depending on the relationship between the individual participants, the physical contact may take the form of gently stroking the shoulder or back in a sensual way, caressing the buttocks, embracing and slowly rubbing the bodies together, or direct gentle genital stimulation by hand, tongue, or mouth.

The purpose of the Communication is to make all the participants aware of their sexual senses and to achieve an initial arousal and sensual energy throughout the Gathering. This initial arousal must not result in impassioned activity, any form of sexual intercourse, or other activities that may result in ejaculation. This is only the beginning of the ritual; its purpose is simply to awaken everyone's sexual awareness. In fact, it's fine if during subsequent successions of the cycle some participants lose their erections or reduce their level of arousal.

At this point the priest or priestess and his or her chosen assistants ensure the initial arousal of the Principal Conduit, who has already been selected and has taken up position on the convocation stone, naked or decoratively adorned. The priest or priestess, with the help of the assistants, caresses the Principal's body, especially the erogenous areas, including the genitals, to ensure the Principal's awareness of sexual arousal. The Principal Conduit may wish to raise the knees by placing the heels next to the buttocks and then part the knees to as

HOW THE SEX
MAGIC RITUAL
WORKS

wide an angle as possible, which exposes the genitalia and anus and enables easier access by the priest or priestess. This position is an ancient reference and can be seen particularly in the Welsh and northern French tradition of exhibitionist carvings (of both males and females) and the Irish Sheela-na-Gig tradition of the similarly exposed female genitalia.

Many individuals who have experienced the role of Principal Conduit say that the very act of exposing their genitalia in such an uncompromising way is sufficient to arouse their sexual awareness even without the additional stimulation provided by the facilitators. You must also be aware that this is an extremely vulnerable position, and from this point onward the Principal Conduit must be treated with the greatest consideration and respect.

If a male has been chosen as the Principal Conduit, he may wish to lie face-down on the convocation stone. Stimulation in this case may begin by easing apart the buttocks and gently blowing on the area around the anus and scrotum. This can be followed by light touching of the same area and caressing of the testicles. At this point the male Principal Conduit usually begins to rotate his pelvis and push his penis against the convocation stone. If he gently lifts his pelvis region, a hand may be inserted between the body and the stone from behind and between the legs, in such a way that the hand gains access to the penis from below and can begin masturbation. This is a favored position for most male Principal Conduits as it allows simultaneous stimulation of the anus and anal areas by the tongue and fingers as the penis is being massaged.

As the Principal Conduit is being caressed, he or she in turn is caressing the priest or priestess and the other assistants gathered around the convocation stone. In this manner mutual stimulation is almost guaranteed.

At this point in the ritual everyone is fully aware of their sexual senses and an initial arousal has been achieved among the participants, the Principal Conduit, the priest or priestess, and the assistants. This arousal is maintained by self-masturbation or by continued contact with other participants in the Gathering.

At this point the Gathering divides into small groups or pairs to prepare for the Augmentation.

AWAKENING

Augmentation

This stage of the cycle allows participants to deepen and broaden their sexual stimulation and sensory experience.

The first step in the Augmentation is to retrieve the spell and reestablish it as the focus of the ritual. To do this, the priest or priestess chants the spell, and it is repeated by the participants of the Gathering. It may well take several repetitions of chanting before the priest or priestess feels that the Gathering is entirely focused on the spell and its intention. At this point the spell is suspended once again in order to bring the focus back to the sensory realm.

The initial sexual stimulation is experienced mainly in a single location deep within the genital region, usually in between the genitals and the anal orifice. This is the area we perceive as the root of our sexual stimulation. This arousal results in a tightening of the muscles in the same region and slow pulses of exquisite sensory pleasure flowing over the whole body.

The purpose of Augmentation is to deepen and broaden this initial sexual awareness by physically stimulating other areas of the body, raising awareness of their pleasure-giving properties and beginning the work of intensifying the eventual orgasm and maximizing the generated energy that will carry the spell. These areas are commonly known as the erogenous zones, though in Druidic tradition their name more closely resembles "augmentation areas."

In females the most intense erogenous areas are the clitoris, the whole area surrounding the entrance to the vagina, and in particular the actual entrance and the areas just inside the orifice. The area surrounding the anus and the passage walls just inside the anus are also considered to be among the most stimulating. Secondary augmentation areas can be found around the nipples, at the nape of the neck, around the ear, along the underside of the whole length of the

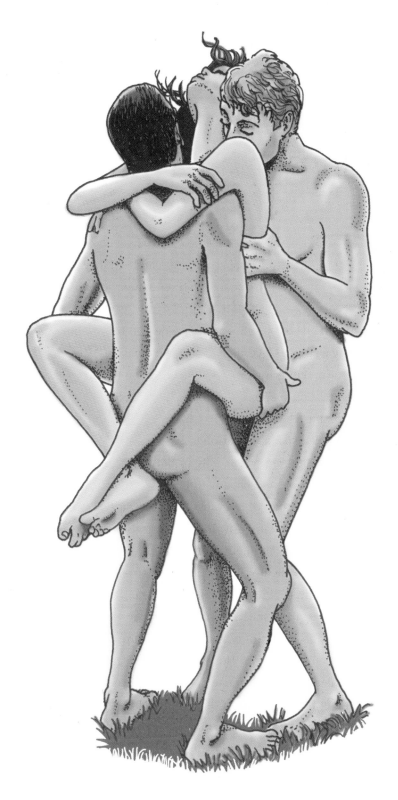

Augmentation begins the work of intensifying the eventual orgasm and maximizing the generated energy that will carry the spell.

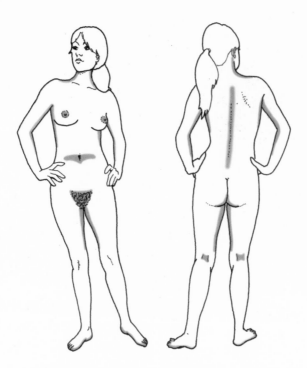

The Augmentation areas of the female body. By careful and controlled stimulation of these areas, sexual excitement may be enhanced and maintained for extraordinarily long periods.

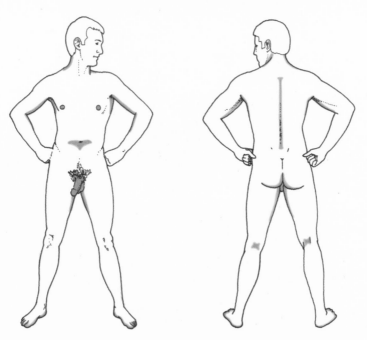

These "Augmentation areas" are now more commonly known as erogenous zones. Druidic lore has known and used these areas of sensory stimulation for millennia.

arm, at the armpit, along each side of the length of the spine, around the stomach, at the area between the vagina and the anus, at the tops of the legs near the vagina, at the backs of the knees, around the toes, and along the sole of the foot.

In males the most intense erogenous areas are the shoulders of the head of the penis, the head of the penis itself, the underside of the entire length of the penis, the area at the top of each leg to each side of the penis, and, as for females, the area of the anus. The secondary augmentation areas listed for females above are equally stimulating to males.

All of these erogenous areas may be stimulated by the fingers, the hand, the tongue, the lips, the mouth, and so on. Males may use their erect penis and females their breasts and erect nipples to stimulate other participants. In some cases participants may also augment stimulation with suitable fetishes, phalluses, and other appropriate objects (see part 1 for information on safety and hygiene).

It may seem very obvious to say, but male penetration of the female can also play a significant role at this stage. Anal penetration is preferred by some females; it may be a solitary act or done in conjunction with another male exercising vaginal penetration. Combinations of male penetration and the use of phalluses and other fetish objects may also be adopted.

Another well-used form of stimulation is that of visual arousal. A large number of today's erotic dances derive from sex magic rituals, and certainly an entire modern-day industry has grown up around the idea of precoital visual stimulation. I have been in Gatherings where a solo female dancer has performed a well-rehearsed erotic dance; where individuals or couples have spontaneously entered the center of the Circle and improvised an erotic performance; and even where a professional "exotic" dancer was hired to perform.

The visual stimulation may not always be aimed at the whole of the Gathering. Individuals may perform erotic events just for their partners. In fact, individuals may often be seen at sex magic Gatherings standing in front of their partner masturbating, exposing themselves in an exhibitionist manner, or performing arousing dances or gyrations.

I believe that there are varying degrees of exhibitionist and voyeuristic tendencies in all of us, and we only need the right circumstances to bring them to

AUGMENTATION

the forefront. Sex magic is an extremely healthy outlet for these tendencies and for exercising the suppressed emotions that are within us all. Venting these emotions can be an enormously exhilarating and gratifying experience and can work as a stabilizing influence on our personality as a whole. It also gives reign to a vast range of creative forces that otherwise may not have such a powerful outlet in our everyday lives.

While some participants are acting out for their partners or the group as a whole, the other participants in the Gathering watch while continuing their own arousal, whether by masturbating, coupling, or some other form of stimulation. Participants may often find themselves involved in a spontaneous rhythmic chanting that reinforces the visual event and synchronizes their own masturbation or mutual stimulation with that of the performers.

This part of the ritual often occupies the Gathering for a considerable length of time. Remember that you are working toward the augmentation and intensification of the eventual orgasm; the more the potential energy of the orgasm can be increased, the better.

It can be seen that Augmentation is perhaps the most sexually creative part of the ritual, giving the opportunity for infinite variations and combinations of sexual stimulation. Experience suggests that different individuals have differently sensitive erogenous zones and respond differently to different stimulation techniques. What works best for an individual can be discovered only through experimentation and, if you have a good memory, at the initiation ritual detailed in part 3.

Both males and females should regularly practice stimulation techniques on themselves, by masturbating in the most creative way possible as well as exploring potential physical and visual stimuli. If they are in a relationship and their partner is a willing participant, they should experiment and practice with their partner to discover the most effective combinations of stimulation techniques.

Individuals who are not in a relationship may be totally dependent upon their involvement with your Gathering to be able to experiment, practice, and develop

Visual stimulation plays a large part in the Augmentation succession. Erotic dance and simulated sex acts are intended to arouse sexual desire and energy among the entire Gathering.

their stimulation techniques. Similarly, few people will be provided with the circumstances to participate in group sexual activities outside of the Gathering.

Two things become apparent here. First, the Gathering must be a strong, secure, trustworthy group of people sharing a clear, common goal, that of mutual learning, experimentation, commitment to each other, and commitment to the fundamentals of the Druidic tradition and sex magic in particular.

Second, there must be some opportunity for training and practice within the group in addition to the formal rituals of the Gathering. Informal weekly gatherings, called indulgences, may be arranged to indulge participants' requests for experimentation and practice. More formal training groups may also convene with a view to exploring new areas of Druidic practice and learning the tradition.

Through this succession of the Projection Cycle you can broaden the sensory stimulation to most parts of the body and make the sexual experience consume the entire body rather than just a single isolated location. As the sensual experience is augmented throughout the body, you get the first sense of leaving the confines of the physical body and of being entirely consumed by the experience. It floods into all the areas of your being and begins to stimulate your internal energy. This is the true beginning of your involvement in the ritual, as this is the very energy you will be using to project your spell.

As the Augmentation continues, it inevitably results in an intensification of the sensations. The length of time it takes to achieve this point is unpredictable; the priest or priestess must judge when this point is reached, and this is when the Intensification succession begins.

In addition to gathering for ritual assemblies, the Gathering would meet with their Druidic priest or priestess on a regular basis to discuss the developing practices of the group and to explore Druidic tradition and practices in general.

Intensification

In Intensification, your sexual sensations are becoming intense but are still controllable. You are still able to move back from that irrevocable point at which your orgasm is both imminent and inevitable.

Recognizing the point of arrival at the threshold of the Intensification is the key to real Augmentation and to maximizing the power of the orgasm. Trained and experienced participants can arrive and retreat from this threshold over and over again, each time increasing the potential of their orgasm and each time reducing the sensitivity of their stimulated areas so that even greater intensification can be achieved.

This process is basically about building up the potential power of the orgasm. Each time the threshold of intensification is reached, the participant learns to relax and retreat from the final commitment to the orgasm.

In practical terms this means a total and immediate control over the means, source, and provider of the stimulation that has brought the participant thus far. If the stimulation is self-masturbation, for example, the participant must practice self-control over that most powerful urge to submit to the ecstasy of the orgasm. This may sound like a simple task, but we must remember that orgasm is one of the most, if not the most, powerful of our human instincts. It remains one of our most primary motivations, deeply seated in the oldest part of our brain. It requires repeated training and intense concentration to exercise even the lowest level of control over this powerful inherited instinct.

Intensification is a fleeting state, a brief transition from the state of Augmentation in which you can feel the rhythm of your stimulation increase, but before the final commitment to orgasm and ejaculation. Developing the ability to

The ability to advance to the threshold, recognize it, sustain and stabilize this heightened level of stimulation, and then retreat from it forms a repeating pattern.

recognize the approach of this state, to control it, and to communicate this control to any others involved in your stimulation is one of the most difficult challenges of sex magic.

Practice is the best means of developing this skill, and self-masturbation is the best means of beginning this practice. With practice and concentration you will learn to achieve all three objectives of Intensifcation at the same time:

- Recognizing the arrival of the orgasm threshold

- Retreating from the commitment to the orgasm

- Maintaining a state of intense arousal without progressing to the commitment to orgasm

For the male, when you learn to identify the threshold of orgasm and gain the self-control to hold back from committing yourself to it, you can stabilize the sensory stimulation by gently massaging the area directly below and underneath the head of the penis. Even by using just one finger and applying gentle pressure to this area, a state of intense sensory pleasure can be maintained for a surprising length of time.

The female may achieve the same results with gentle massage of the clitoris, nipples, and vaginal area.

Individuals will have their preferred area of stimulation. The ones mentioned above are general suggestions. Every person must learn the intricacies of his or her own body. Experiment, explore, and practice. Accept no barriers. Your body is your own, and unfortunately most are unexplored territories. I am still constantly surprised by how little some people know about their own bodies and how reluctant some can be to explore and experiment with their sensory capacities.

The ability to advance to the threshold, recognize it, sustain and stabilize this heightened level of stimulation, and then retreat from it forms a repeating pattern. Forward, stabilize, retreat, then repeat, time and time again, with the experience intensifying each time.

HOW THE SEX
MAGIC RITUAL
WORKS

It is the objective of the experienced priest and priestess to synchronize this pattern among the individuals and subgroups of the Gathering in order to encourage participants' orgasms to coincide. The Gathering's communal orgasm generates energy in the most intense and powerful manner.

Once you have gained some acceptable level of self-control over these events, and this will take substantial practice, it becomes important to extend this control to others. This means being able to communicate to someone else effectively enough that they are able to exercise the same level of control over your sensory stimulation as you can yourself. If you have a committed relationship this development is made simpler by your close relationship with your partner.

The inevitable consequence of hovering on the threshold of commitment to your orgasm is that, at some point, whether through personal choice, instruction from the priest or priestess facilitating the Gathering, or simple loss of self-control or the control of others who are stimulating you, you will find yourself at that very brief moment when you have given in to your basic instincts and you are irrevocably committed to the orgasm.

Quickening

The Quickening is the moment of self-awareness that extends from that instant when you know that your orgasm is both imminent and inevitable up until the first convulsive ejaculation that marks the all-important moment of orgasm and projection. It is the moment when you can finally let yourself be carried away on the sheer ecstasy and unbridled pleasure of your orgasm.

Or is it?

The answer is both yes and no, because this is also the moment when you prepare yourself for the duality of the orgasm.

Of course it is important that you submit yourself to the intense pleasure and stimulation of the final moments that lead up to your orgasm, but at the same time you must not forget the prime reason for originating the orgasm and the purpose of the ritual itself. Amid the chaos of emotions and sensory excitement of the fast-approaching orgasm, you must direct yourself to retrieve the spell, incantation, or intention that you have suspended, return it to the forefront of your consciousness, and prepare it for projection into the collective energy, where it begins its journey to the intended recipient.

As you will see, this requires immense concentration. Every ounce of your being will want to concern itself only with the approaching orgasm; all of your consciousness will want to focus on the anticipation of the ecstatic pleasure about to consume you.

However, you must wrench your conscious awareness away from its preoccupation with your sensory pleasure, leaving your physical body to cope with

The imaginary glass sheet passing through the male (or female) body. This separates the sensual ecstasy of the lower part of the body from the spiritual consciousness of the upper during the Quickening succession.

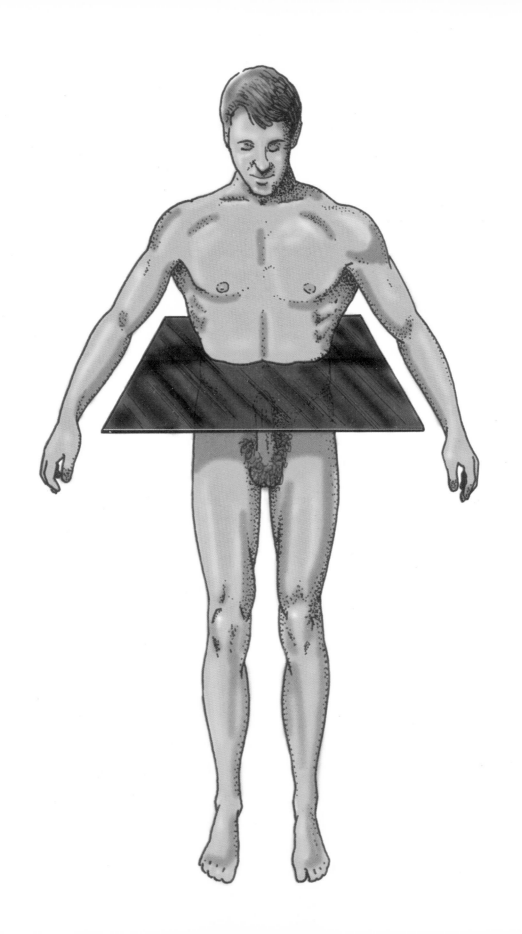

the little remaining time you have before ejaculation. You must now focus your mind on retrieving your spell from its suspended state and reaffirming it before attaching it to your internal generated energy.

This is a very difficult task, given that the approaching orgasm is physically all-consuming, and it requires prolonged and repeated practice. Again, self-masturbation is the favored method for practicing and developing this technique.

Passing the threshold of the Quickening is one of the more easily recognized progressions of the Projection Cycle. Apart from the overwhelming internal experience, external indicators become apparent. These will include, in the male, an even greater stiffening of the erect penis, a tightening of the scrotum, a raising of the testicles, and a general tightening of the body's muscular structure, often resulting in the arching of the back and the projection forward of the pelvic area. This is often accompanied by the clenching of the buttocks and sometimes rhythmic thrusting of the pelvic area, simulating sexual intercourse.

In the female, you can witness nearly all the appropriate similarities, together with a pronounced tightening of the inner thigh muscles, either a spreading of the legs apart or a clenching of the legs together, and a firmer erection of the nipples.

In both male and female vocal indicators can be heard, ranging from quiet anticipatory moans and a quickening in the breathing to wild ecstatic screams and convulsive groans.

Whichever indicators are observed, it becomes very obvious that the individual is, at this stage, completely committed to the orgasm.

During this physically all-consuming stage of the cycle, how do we exercise any control whatsoever over our conscious mind?

In answer, I will once again return to the simple tactics of my early training.

The first stage of the technique, which, as noted earlier, requires lengthy practice, is to learn to identify when you have reached the threshold of the Quickening. Passing this point commits you to the orgasm. You eventually learn to recognize the internal experience and the external physical indicators that confirm your imminent ejaculation. If stimulation to this point has been achieved by penetration, this is the moment when the penis is withdrawn.

When you reach this point, make a conscious effort to "let go" of the mental experience and allow your physical body to continue the orgasm. It is a difficult experience to explain. You must shift the sensory focus from the mind to the genitals, allowing that area to lead the orgasm, while also numbing the sensory center in the mind.

I was taught to visualize a glass sheet or board passing into my body just above the navel, isolating the lower sensory area from the upper, at the very moment of entering the Quickening. Like a painless guillotine, the sheet or board cuts off the physical sensual pleasure of the orgasm and ejaculation from the upper level of awareness and spiritual consciousness.

Imagining a guillotine bisecting your body may seem a strange concept, but it works, and in turn it signifies the deeper concept involved: the "duality" of the orgasm.

This, then, is the first stage of this particular training regime: letting the physical body experience the progress to ejaculation while the conscious awareness, at this stage, is just suspended. Once this part of the technique is mastered—and this will take some time—the next stage is to do the same thing, only this time using the conscious awareness to focus on another topic, such as your spell.

Different people have suggested to me various ways of doing this. Some subscribe to the bodily division technique described above; others suggest a rapid alternation technique, whereby the consciousness alternates rapidly between the sensory and the rational; still others suggest a "double plane" scenario, where both sensation and reason exist on two planes of the same continuum. This double plane scenario may be likened to a mid-ocean view of the sea and sky. It encompasses all the visionary field and divides it into two planes that exist simultaneously. If we imagine the sensory experience of the orgasm as one plane (the sea) and the conscious awareness focusing on the spell as the other (the sky), both can exist simultaneously, occupying one's entire focus and progressing together toward the end of the journey.

This technique involves extensive training and practice. In simple terms, it is like playing the piano, where both hands do entirely different things at the same time. The pianist can switch the focus of his or her attention to either hand without the other hand's performance suffering, playing the melody with one

QUICKENING

hand and the accompaniment with the other. Anyone who has sat and listened to a classical concert pianist or an inspired jazz pianist and wondered how so many different notes could come from the hands of only one performer has begun to understand the potential of this technique.

There are, I am sure, many other techniques, and you may even wish to develop a personal technique of your own.

Whichever methodology you develop or adopt, the purpose is the same, that is, to reinforce the physical experience with conscious awareness, and to reinforce the potency of the conscious awareness with the physical power of the orgasm, while at the same time being aware that both are separate experiences. The mental and the physical are together yet apart, mutually dependent but experienced independently, each an equal half of the duality.

Though it may seem unlikely when you first begin, eventually, after sufficient practice, this process of duality becomes second nature, and you will be able to switch between the sensual and the spiritual consciousness at will, suspending one while focusing on the other. Having achieved this level of control, it is then time to return to the ritual and the Projection Cycle and apply what you have learned.

As you submit to the inevitable progress of the Quickening, the body is assigned the physical or sensual experience while the consciousness has the task of retrieving the suspended spell and bringing it to the forefront of awareness, where it remains until the next succession arrives. This succession, of course, is the pinnacle of both the Projection Cycle and the ritual as a whole: the orgasm and Projection.

Orgasm and Projection

If the thought has crossed your mind that exercising such a degree of self-control during the Quickening is a difficult and challenging task, then the idea of doing the same during the convulsive ecstasy of orgasm might just seem impossible. But the fact is that with practice and patience, you will develop your self-control and conscious awareness to a level where this is an achievable goal.

In the Quickening, you separate the sensual physical experience from the spiritual consciousness. Once this duality is achieved and stabilized, it continues along, with your focus shifting between the two parts, until you feel the first contraction of the orgasm.

At this point—never before or after—the two elements are brought together, bound, and projected. The physical orgasm and the spell carried in the conscious awareness, when bonded together, become your personal generated energy. This unique creation will be both the vehicle and the protector of your spell, incantation, or intention on its journey through the collective energy to its recipient.

Knowing that this is your goal will give you insight into the training and discipline needed to achieve it.

First, let's look at the initial contractions of the orgasm itself.

The Quickening brought you to the point of the first contraction. You experienced the internal and external indicators that signal the imminent release of the first and most powerful projection of your orgasm, and you have separated the two elements of the duality. You should be confident in your ability to control the Projection Cycle up to this point; only when you have mastered this stage should you progress to the next.

The point of projection of the spell, utilizing the intense power of the orgasm. The spell begins its visualized journey to its recipient, in this case being carried by the visualized dove messenger.

This next step involves binding the spell to the projected energy through focus and visualization. Your body and mind will both naturally want to submit to the ecstasy of the orgasm at the cost of all other sensation and awareness. It is your task to develop the control to overcome these natural instincts.

Exercising your newly refined awareness and self-control, call forth the first part of your visualization just prior to the orgasm. The visualization begins with an image of the potential generated energy being built up in your body and about to be released through your orgasm.

This image may take any form that complements your preexisting visualization of the collective energy. Of course, it must also take a form that will be suitable for you to bind your spell, incantation, or intention to. Its form may also be influenced by the content of the spell itself.

Some people, for example, visualize their generated energy as an arrow with the spell tied to it as a small note. The arrow leaves the tip of the penis or emerges from the vagina with immense power and energy at the moment of the orgasm's initial contraction, carrying the spell on its journey to the recipient.

Others visualize their generated energy as a white dove with the spell, written on a small piece of parchment, held within its beak.

One individual told me that, when projecting a spell to an infant, she had visualized her generated energy as a tiny, beautifully colored butterfly emerging from her vagina with her spell contained within the decorations of its wings. When the butterfly completed its journey through an idyllic visualization of the collective energy, it bound its spell to the sleeping infant by flapping its wings, thereby loosening the spell in the form of a cloud of sparkling dust that fell upon the sleeping child.

I could continue with innumerable examples of my own visualizations or with those described to me by others, but I am sure you can already see that each visualization is unique, reflecting the personality of its creator and the purpose for which it is intended. Some are gentle and ethereal, others are vivid and powerful, still others are dark and profound, having arisen from deep concern and anxiety. Sometimes the choice of an appropriate visualization is difficult; on other occasions it becomes immediately apparent. Only you will know what is appropriate for your purpose.

The important point here is that the visualization must be explored well before the ritual begins, as soon as you become aware of the spell and its purpose. There is little point in getting to this very sensitive yet powerful stage of the cycle and then attempting to create an instant visualization.

Using the meditation technique described in part 1, focus your concentration on the intent and recipient of the spell and explore potential visualization options. Eventually an appropriate one will become apparent. Develop your initial interpretation of the visualization until you have refined it sufficiently, then memorize it. In this way you will not be dependent upon sublime inspiration at the very point of ejaculation.

As you approach the moment of ejaculation, reunite the elements of the duality and bind your spell to the projected energy in a way that most suits your visualization. On the first pulse of the ejaculation, your visualization begins.

ORGASM AND
PROJECTION

There is, incidentally, no reason to suppress your orgasm by focusing only upon the visualization. In fact, the very opposite is true. You have, throughout the ritual, been building and intensifying the potential of your orgasm. Continue to work toward this end. Exaggerate the pulses and bodily movements that go with it. Use vocalization to amplify the power of the experience. Work with your partner or other members of your group with a view to maximizing your potential and the potential of the others. Open your mind to as many ideas as possible, and don't forget to enjoy the pleasure of the experience.

In some cases, but certainly not all cases, all the participants will be oriented in the same direction at the moment of initial ejaculation, and an attempt to synchronize the ejaculation may be made.

In most cases, participants will bring themselves to the point of ejaculation by self-masturbating or doing the same for another participant, who will in turn be masturbating them. No one will ejaculate while penetrating.

Males usually stand to ejaculate. They may take advantage of this position to augment the power of the orgasm by thrusting their hips forward to dispatch the generated energy on its journey. This can, of course, also be done from the lying down, seated, or crouching position. It is purely a matter of individual choice.

Females, in my experience, generally prefer to lie down or crouch, sometimes while using phalluses, fetish objects, and even electronic vibrators as a means of greater stimulation.

The female may, given the right circumstances, also achieve this ritual orgasm while being penetrated by one or more males, but it is important that none of the males achieve ejaculation while inserted, as this defies one of the prime principles. For this reason, this method is unsuitable for rituals where a synchronized orgasm is the objective.

The initial pulse of your orgasm will be followed by a series of successive pulses, which you use to reinforce the main ejaculation. Your visualization, of course, should be designed to incorporate these successive pulses.

As the intensity of your orgasm begins to subside, your focus can begin to concentrate more singularly on your visualization. At this point you cross the threshold to the Continuance succession.

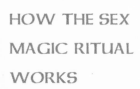

An important consideration that must not be overlooked in your preparation or during the actual ritual itself is the physical manifestation of the ejaculation. Every individual involved in the ritual will experience the convulsive spasms of the orgasm. If the ritual is facilitated with total success, all will be experiencing it at the same time. You will appreciate that this will not be the time to be remembering complex rules or to be preoccupied with considerations outside your immediate sensory involvement.

So there are two things you need to sort out well before you begin: making arrangements to ensure the physical well-being of all the participants, and what to do about all the bodily fluids that will inevitably be generated.

Making sure that the Circle is large enough to accommodate the number of individuals involved in the ritual can assist the first of these considerations. Bear in mind that participants will each need enough room to stand, sit, and lie. They will inevitably also form into small or medium-sized groups during the ritual, and your Circle must be able to accommodate these groupings.

Make sure that all the participants are fully aware of any potential dangers arising from their body adornments before the ritual begins. I have witnessed a number of painful accidents involving piercings, nipple rings, vaginal rings, and chains as well as incidents of breathing problems resulting from neck chokers. These dangers will quickly be lost from the minds of the participants as the ritual gains impetus.

Also make note of the potential dangers of using phalluses and other instruments or fetishes that may be inserted into the body. Consideration of size, shape, and material of manufacture must be taken into account by all those involved. What "fits" one individual may not always be suitable for another.

A short conversation facilitated by the priest or priestess before the ritual begins will serve the purpose of informing everyone present of what is being proposed for use and will give everyone the opportunity to ask questions, comment, and state their individual point of view before any commitment is made.

As far as bodily fluids are concerned, it seems that everyone nowadays is well aware of the dangers entailed in the exchange or transfer of bodily fluids. Safety and hygiene are paramount concerns, but there are a significant number

of people who find the whole matter of what they consider to be sticky, messy substances totally distasteful. As is the way of things, there are of course others who find the very same fluids attractive and stimulating.

We therefore have to take a sympathetic path.

Nearly all the groups I have been involved with consider safety and hygiene to be of utmost important. I therefore recommend the use of condoms by all male participants in order to gather and secure the bulk of the fluids concerned. The availability of sufficient and adequate hygienic wipes for everyone's use is also essential. It may also be useful to have a supply of surgical or household gloves on hand, as someone inevitably ends up cleaning the area afterward.

All you can really avoid by exercising the utmost caution and applying the most stringent hygiene standards is the *unwitting* contact with bodily fluids. The element of exposure by choice is entirely up to the individual concerned. What is of prime importance is that all the participants are fully aware of all the risks and dangers involved and that they are able to make their own informed decisions about the terms of their own involvement.

It should be someone's responsibility to make sure there are adequate sanitary waste bags available so that everyone can dispose of their condoms, wipes, and so on. This is an especially important consideration if your ritual is facilitated outdoors; the last thing you would wish to do is violate the natural setting or damage the environment with litter or any other form of contamination.

Continuance

This succession can be explained quite simply as the period when subtle sexual stimulation is used to fuel the visualization of the generated energy's journey to the recipient. The stimulation can, as in other parts of the ritual, be produced by self-masturbation or by the involvement of another individual. The intention is to maintain not the ecstatic peak of the orgasm, but the gentle elation that follows the intense power of the ejaculation, thereby sustaining the visualization.

Care should be taken to avoid stimulation of sensitive areas. The orgasm leaves certain parts of the body in an extremely sensitive and excited state. Sometimes just the touch of a finger or even the accidental brush of a piece of clothing in one of these areas can send an electrifying jolt through the entire body. This phenomenon can be exploited in the appropriate situation, but it must be avoided at all costs during the Continuance succession. The intensity of the impulse created will distract the individual from his or her visualization, negating the purpose of the ritual.

In the male the areas most likely to produce distracting sensations are the upper surface of the head of the penis, the nape of the neck, the ears, and the underside of the arms, particularly around the armpit.

In the female, these areas include the entire area surrounding the clitoris as well as the nape of the neck, the ears, and the underside of the arms, particularly around the armpit.

By practicing on your own body and on others, you will soon become aware of both the overly sensitive areas and those parts of the body that may be gently stimulated without producing distracting sensations. The object is to provide yourself or your partner(s) with sufficient stimulation to maintain the sense of

Wrapped in the mantle of your secure place where the ritual is being facilitated and fueled by the sublime sensations of the stimulation you are experiencing, your visualized journey continues.

"otherworldliness" and fuel the visualization without producing sensations so powerful that they become distracting or disruptive.

There are a number of established techniques used to produce the desired level of stimulation, but be aware that these will differ among individuals, and there is no substitute for exploration and discovery of your own body and your partner's.

I suggest that you begin by trying the following and build your repertoire from there.

For the male. The partner kneels between the legs of the male, places the semi-erect penis on the male's stomach, and, using either the tongue or the fingers, gently stimulates the underside of the penis along its entire length.

At the same time the partner either caresses the testicles with one hand while using the extended fingers of this hand to also massage the anus, or caresses the nipples and the chest area. The partner may also alternate between these areas.

Gentle rhythmic penetration of the anus and massage of the entrance of the anus is also effective, as is the massage of the inner thighs and feet.

For the female. The partner kneels between the legs of the female and, using the fingers or the tongue, gently stimulates the lower area of the vagina, the area between the vagina and the anus, and/or the anus itself. If this is done by using the tongue, both hands may be used to spread open the vagina, giving greater access and more control. If this is done by using the fingertips, then the thumbs may be used to massage the anal area and the area between the vagina and the anus.

Care should be exercised in stimulating the nipples, as these become very sensitive following the orgasm.

In general terms, if the areas around the genitals are being gently stimulated (avoiding the over-sensitive points), massage of the rest of the body serves to reinforce the pleasurable sensations produced. Scented oils and potions massaged into the body also assist in maintaining the state of consciousness necessary to continue the visualized journey.

If you are conducting the ritual on your own, no one will know better than you the areas of the body and the strength of stimulation that serves your purpose best.

The purpose of stimulation in the Continuance is to fuel the visualized journey of your generated energy. You will remember from part 1 that the journey of the generated energy has been well planned in advance. You have already visualized this journey a number of times in preparation for this moment.

So, wrapped in the mantle of your secure place where the ritual is being facilitated and fueled by the sublime sensations of the stimulation you are experiencing, your visualization of the journey continues.

The generated energy, in whatever form you now perceive it, bursts from your body, projected by the concentrated power of your orgasm, and makes its way through the enormity of the collective energy. Perhaps it is the speeding arrow, a lightning bolt, a bird, or a tiny butterfly. Whatever its manifestation, it progresses without obstruction through the entry portal, through the collective energy, through the exit portal, and finally on to its destination, the recipient.

This journey can be as short or as long as you desire. There are no rules; you are in complete control of the entire event. It is your generated energy, your spell, your visualization, and your choice of recipient, and it is your consciousness that provides the power.

Make this a positive experience. Remember, this is all of your own making. If you plan the visualization carefully, know by heart every detail, construct your spell or incantation with only good intention, and exercise your knowledge of the duality and projection to best effect, then this will be a life-enriching experience for both you and the recipient.

Your journey so far has brought your spell, carried by your generated energy, to its destination, the recipient or, in some cases, the collective energy itself.

The next step is to bind the spell to its recipient.

This can be done in whatever way pleases you. The gentle dropping of dust from the wings of a butterfly was perfectly suited to the example discussed earlier. Many people visualize the spell as ivy and bind it to the recipient. Another common visualization is that of a fragile mantle or gossamer cloth being first laid over and then absorbed by the recipient's body, thereby taking the spell into the very being of the recipient. Again, the choice is yours, and you may vary it on every occasion and adapt it to best suit the circumstances.

When the spell is targeted toward the collective energy, the journey finishes at the energy source you have already placed at the center of your visualization. You will remember the shrub my grandfather described to me in my youth. In my experience, and in that others have shared with me, this core energy is of such immense power that it would be inconceivable to enter it. Therefore, binding your spell to the energy source will usually involve a visualization of throwing or pitching the generated energy into the source, witnessing the spell entering (as in the case of an arrow or a bird), leaving the spell at the threshold of the core, such as on an altar stone, in a receptacle of some sort, or just simply at the entrance to the core.

Then stand back and allow the core to absorb the spell. Take care not to visualize this as too powerful an event. The core should carefully and peacefully absorb the generated energy and the spell. Avoid destructive images, such as great flames of energy consuming your carrier or massive hands brutally grabbing your fragile small bird. These sorts of images suggest the destruction of your spell, not its absorption.

Develop a visualization that leaves you confident that its recipient, whether an individual or the core energy, has absorbed your spell and taken it to heart. Your main reward is the sense of well-being created by this conscious giving of beneficial influence. Your entire being must believe that your efforts are contributing to a successful outcome; if your belief ebbs, so will the power of your influence and the effectiveness of your efforts.

When you are confident that the spell is inseparably linked to its recipient, begin your visualized journey back through the collective energy.

Every visualized journey you make through or into the collective energy provides you with the opportunity to explore it and build in more detail. One of the many aspects you may wish to create in it is a place of meditation.

I have met many people, particularly those living in cities, busy urban environments, and even simply chaotic homes, who find that having a peaceful meditation place in the collective energy that they can access through a visualized journey is extremely beneficial.

This place can be whatever you want it to be. It will end up as one of a collection of places within your visualization of the collective energy. Each one will be created for a special purpose and will have unique features. You can create these places as the need arises by using the tranquil meditation technique described in part 1, a technique that by now you should be well on the road to mastering.

Once again, do not leave the creation of these places until the very moment you intend to use them. Try to plan ahead. If you have some spare time, try to anticipate and build the sorts of places you might enjoy having in your visualization space. Especially try to envision the types of places you might need in times of stress or trouble. Your self-awareness and consciousness will not be at its most creative when you are under pressure. Prepare these places in advance,

explore them, and add detail to them so that when they are needed they are ready to provide you with the environment that reflects your needs.

You will have gathered by now that each person's visualization of the collective energy is unique to him or her. Some individuals choose to keep their visualizations secret, while others derive great pleasure from sharing their creations with other individuals.

You will also by now appreciate that the collective energy occupies an infinite space, allowing you to create as many special places in it as you desire. It has only two boundaries: the two portals through which you enter and leave it. These are necessary for you to make your journey. Both these portals are movable. You may take your entry portal with you to whatever location you wish, while your exit portal shifts in relation to the recipient of your spell.

On your return journey, having securely bound the spell to your recipient and witnessed its absorption, you may choose to visit one of these places and spend some time meditating. This will depend on a number of circumstances, including:

- The energy level your body is able to maintain. If the ritual so far has been particularly strenuous or energetic, you may feel tired.

- The time span of your journey so far. It may be that you have taken a complex route to your recipient and feel the need to return to your physically conscious state.

- Reduction in stimulation. The sustained stimulation fueling your visualization may be ebbing, and you may feel that you can no longer maintain your visualization.

The reasons for returning directly through the collective energy's exit portal are many, but on some occasions, when things may be going just right, you may choose to lodge in one of your meditation spaces for a short while and contemplate what you have achieved (and hope to achieve) by your journey.

Evaluating what has happened and how you can work to improve it are very important elements of your development. No one does everything perfectly every time, and self-criticism can provide you with both the motivation and the information necessary for you to improve and refine your techniques.

This meditative process develops maturity in your practices and workings. Take the time to challenge yourself, your attitudes, and your actions as often as you can. It can and will make you both a better Druid and a better person.

Inevitably, at some point, your energy or the sustained stimulation of the Continuance will begin to fade, and you will have to journey back through the collective energy's portal to return to your conscious physical state. Once you feel firmly embedded back in your body, it is important that you continue the Projection Cycle through its last succession, that of Relaxation.

Relaxation

Your return to conscious awareness may initially leave you in a confused state, but there are a number of practical issues you will need to give your immediate attention to.

You will now want to bring to a halt the stimulation that has been powering your visualization in the Continuance succession. If you have been stimulating yourself, you may well find that you stopped without realizing it during your return journey. Otherwise, gradually slow your self-stimulation until you arrive comfortably at an agreeable halt.

If another person has been providing the stimulation, communicate to him or her in a soft, unhurried manner that you wish to cease the stimulation and return to a relaxed state. This may take a little while and require you to exercise patience and consideration. Remember that those individuals who have been maintaining stimulation will not have had as productive a time as those who have taken a visualized journey. Their role has been to fuel your task, and they may now want to experience further sexual stimulation themselves. If this is the case you need to be sympathetic to their needs and allow them some degree of indulgence.

Like many other areas of sex magic, this is not without its difficulties.

Having experienced the arousal and stimulation of the orgasm, many people find further sexual activities distasteful. What had previously been exciting and stimulating now seems unnecessary, disagreeable, or even repulsive. The more extreme the sexual activity has been, the more distasteful it may now appear.

In addition, every individual has a different capacity for sexual activity. Some people's sexual appetite is far greater than others', in the same way that one person's stamina may far outstrip another's.

Your return to the conscious awareness of the world around you.

What you may now be faced with is a gathering of people all at various stages of completion of the ritual.

This is another reason to work toward synchronizing the progress toward and through orgasm.

The one thing that you must try to avoid at all cost is the casual and unplanned breaking up of the Gathering as some people, having completed their involvement, try to remove themselves while others are still fully engrossed in the ritual. The slow, time-consuming Relaxation succession aids in this.

As individuals emerge from the Continuance, they begin the process of relaxation, which entails gentle massage, subtle body contact, conscious muscular relaxation, and controlled breathing; all assist the body in returning to its relaxed state. Muscle stretching, head rotation, and neck and shoulder relaxation further help in a slow and gentle return to the everyday world. They also give a focus to those people who emerge from the Projection and Continuance successions of the ritual earlier than others.

This stage of the ritual inevitably sees participants striking up quiet conversations with each other, tentatively moving around the Circle to join other participants, coming together in small groups, and so on. Generally these individuals will involve themselves in activities that will remove their focus from the individuals still immersed in the ritual.

Slowly the individuals who have completed their Projection Cycle come together in a more social way. This group will grow as more and more people complete their cycle, until eventually, all the Gathering is grouped together. If at this stage there are still a few individuals who have what appear to be insatiable sexual appetites, it will be necessary for the priest or priestess, with a few well-chosen words, to curtail their overly enthusiastic efforts.

This then marks the completion of the Projection Cycle. You and the other participants in the Gathering will now be experiencing an all-consuming feeling of well-being; a feeling of having successfully completed a significant task; having undertaken an important journey and returned safely; having created a beneficial influence for individuals and the world; having changed the collective energy through your own efforts and as a result of your own motivation.

Add to this the well-known post-coital "afterglow" and you will feel the need to celebrate your success. To serve this need and the likely need for food and drink (few things give you an appetite comparable to sex magic rituals), we now partake of the final libation of the ritual.

RELAXATION

Final Libation

The priest or priestess speaks a short thanksgiving before beginning the libation to acknowledge the pleasure, excitement, and fulfillment experienced by the individuals of the Gathering. He or she acknowledges the power of the ritual you have all just undertaken and gives thanks for the safe return of those individuals who have made the journey through the collective energy.

Once this is done, everyone puts their clothing back on. This is particularly appreciated if the ritual has been facilitated outdoors.

On this occasion the libation usually consists of food, often bread or cake prepared especially for the occasion, and drink, usually in the form of hot metheglin laced with spirit. The administration of the libation is discussed in more detail in part 3.

Participants normally sit within the Circle to offer and take the libation. Traditionally, both food and drink are passed around the Circle from one participant to another, each taking sufficient for him- or herself and offering the remainder to the next individual.

This is the social time of the ritual. The level of conversation rises, stories are told, songs are sung, poems are recited, and sometimes a little music and dance crops up. You will find it always becomes a very wholesome affair, full of good will and joy. It is the time when tentative arrangements for the next Gathering may be discussed or points of lore and tradition debated.

If the final libation is not controlled to some degree, it will go on all day and night. Eventually, the priest or priestess will call everyone together for the Scattering.

The Scattering

Before the Circle is reopened and the Gathering scatters the priest or priestess issues the farewell. All the participants in the Gathering shake hands with each other, embrace, and wish their colleagues farewell. The accurate translation from the Welsh would be to wish your colleagues "big sails," which demonstrates the seafaring nature of the Welsh tradition.

Having judged that the Gathering is ready to scatter, the priest or priestess removes the dagger sealing the portal to the Circle, partly draws the dagger from its sheath, then slams it closed again, saying, "And so it ends." This phrase marks the completion of the ritual, and the participants depart through the Circle's portal.

When the ritual is facilitated outdoors, it is often held in a grove of trees. On these occasions participants may choose to tie a wish ribbon or spell ribbon to the branch of a tree in the grove as they leave. These ribbons are tied to the tree branch as the wish or spell is spoken, thereby binding the wish or spell to nature and the collective energy. This ritual is the origin of the tradition of tying yellow ribbons to trees as a wish for the safe return of a loved one.

Some individuals choose to tie "crane bags" to branches or place them in nooks in the tree. These bags contain items of import that have been the subject of the individual workings and intentions. The items they contain are charged with the individual's energies with the intention of effecting a change.

There are two points to bear in mind in relation to these practices. First, as Druids and conservationists we do not want to promote littering or defacement of the environment. Make sure that all participants use only natural materials for their ribbons and bags. Apart from being much more in tune with the effort to commune with nature and the collective energy, natural materials are, for the greater part,

This blackthorn tree stands at the edge of the Seven Sisters stone circle in Kerry, Ireland. The practice of tying wish ribbons and crane bags to trees as a means of binding wishes, spells, and intentions is a very old one, but as can be seen from this picture, it is still practiced in Ireland today. These ribbons and crane bags were already tied to the Blackthorn when my Gathering arrived, so we are obviously not the only group using this particular ancient circle.

biodegradable, and in time they will be consumed by the natural environment.

Second, be aware that leaving these ribbons and bags as witness to your ritual may draw unwanted attention to your efforts. This may cause problems in some cases; only you will know your exact circumstances in this regard.

Whether or not they choose to tie wish ribbons, spell ribbons, or crane bags to a branch as they depart, eventually all the participants disperse. The priest or priestess and his or her assistants now have the task of dismantling the ritual setting and erasing the Circle.

First all the ritual equipment is cleansed, as described in part 3. Once cleansed, the equipment is removed from the Circle through the portal. When the Circle is empty, it will be erased. This too will be discussed in detail in part 3.

The final act is the Gift.

The Gift

If you are the facilitating priest or priestess, you are now alone at the site of the Circle where your ritual took place. All the events of the ritual are behind you. You have learned from the experience, as has everyone else involved. You have influenced the collective energy, the recipient of your spell or intention, the other individuals involved, and the site upon which the ritual took place.

Tradition demands that you now leave Nature a gift to acknowledge the power of the forces you worked with and as a token of your respect for the eternal collective energy. This gift must be small in size, of little worldly value, and drawn from a natural source. Appropriate examples include a single small flower, a single sprig of herb, a drop of cleansed springwater, a few crumbs of the bread or cake used in the ritual, or a few drops of the liquid libation used. Anything of this kind would suit.

Cleansing and Purifying Your Cache

When the ritual is over, the Circle has been erased, you have presented the Gift, and you have brought home all the Druidic tools, cloths, vessels, and accessories—what we normally refer to collectively as your cache—you need once again to cleanse them.

The cleansing done at the end of the ritual serves only to prepare your cache to be removed from the protection of the Circle. You now need to cleanse, reenergize, and purify your cache in preparation for storage. You will also need to work a spell of protection upon your cache as you will most likely be storing it outside the protection of a cast Circle.

As you develop and grow in your role as a Celtic sex magic priest or priestess, your cache of tools will grow along with you. Not only will you be continually adding new tools, equipment, and accessories to your cache, but you will be refining and nurturing the ones you already have.

Caches represent and reflect the personality of the individuals who have created them. Few things can tell you as much about a person as the collection of items that make up his or her cache.

Most people begin quite simply and put together a small collection of the tools necessary to begin the basic workings. Simple tools for a simple beginning; that is exactly what I was taught as a young man.

My first tool was a rude wand. For months this was the only tool I possessed. A rude wand is a branch that, after being cleansed, is used in its raw state, thereby maintaining the sap energy and attributes of its donor tree in a "young and unsophisticated" (hence "rude") energy form. Rude wands are usually used only for a brief period, as their energy and attributes are generally considered to have but a brief lifetime. They are used for light, openhearted, fertile workings, such as initiations, springtime bonding, and early morning rituals. They frequently are harvested just before the ritual that they are intended to be used for and are usually left behind, along with the Gift, upon the completion of the working.

My first rude wand, however, stayed with me for months, and I used it repeatedly during that time for all of my early efforts. All the same, it was with this rude wand that I was taught all the techniques of cleansing, purification, protection, and storage that we will examine in this section.

Cleansing Versus Purifying

Before we delve into the specifics of the cleansing working, I will take a little time to discuss the difference between cleansing and purification. I will have to start by confessing that, once again, these words are poor translations from the Welsh, and the subtle difference between the two is lost in the translation.

Cleansing is defined in the Oxford English Dictionary (seventh edition) as "to make clean or pure"; purification is defined as "to cleanse or make pure" but with the added comment, "to make ceremonially clean; to clear of extraneous elements."

In the context of Druidic ritual, cleansing is the physical act of cleaning the items concerned. It is achieved by various physical methods, such as washing, sterilizing, polishing, and so on, and not always in a ceremonial forum.

Purification is the cleansing of the energy and power of the items concerned, or the removal of any negative or otherwise unwanted influences and contamination. It is a mystical, magical activity that is always conducted through ritual and ceremony.

Cleansing Your Cache

The cleansing of your cache is vitally important when the cache has been involved in a sex magic ritual. If your cache is not kept immaculately clean, you are exposing yourself and the rest of your Gathering to the possibility of infection, which can range from simple stomach upset to sexually transmitted diseases. Cleansing is a task that must be undertaken with the utmost fastidiousness. Every item must be thoroughly cleaned prior to storage and then cleaned again when it is taken out of storage for use in a ritual.

The best way to tackle this task is to make a written list of all the items in your cache, from the largest, most useful items right down to the smallest, most insignificant pieces. The idea, of course, is to make sure that you miss absolutely nothing. Work through the entire list in a methodical manner every time you undertake a cleansing. If some items on the list have not been used for a ritual, take them from your storage area and include them in the cleansing and purification rituals anyway. None of your cache can be cleaned too often; take every opportunity to handle, cleanse, purify, and energize all of the items you have accumulated.

The actual cleansing process and the cleansing agents you use will vary according to the individual items of your cache. Common sense and good hygiene will be your watchwords.

A range of herbs, barks, flowers, mosses, seaweeds, and other natural materials are used as effective cleansing agents in Druidic tradition. Even though modern-day science has confirmed that many of these agents actually do contain antiseptic and sterilizing properties, they can rarely be compared to their modern counterparts.

As I have said a number of times, Druidic tradition has always been open to accepting and absorbing contemporary discoveries and using every possible modern practice that does not undermine its basic philosophies. I have no hesitation, therefore, in recommending that you use the most appropriate modern cleansing and sterilizing agents you can find. If in any doubt as to which is the most effective and reliable, contact your local pharmacist, who will always be pleased to advise you on matters of hygiene.

In addition to cleansing agents you will also need polishing agents, which will be used to enhance the cosmetic appearance of the items of your cache. Again, there are traditional agents that may be used, but once more I recommend that you employ whatever modern products are appropriate for this purpose.

Having gathered about you all the necessary cleansing agents, polishing agents, and cleaning cloths, you can begin the cleansing process.

As this is not a formal ritual, I normally do my entire cache cleansing in the kitchen using all the same equipment and agents I use for household cleaning. My cauldron, libation vessels, and candleholders get put in the dishwasher. The covering cloths from my working stone and convocation stone go into the laundry machine, along with any cleansing cloths or other fabric items that I have in my cache. I am perfectly content to let these labor-saving machines bear the brunt of the work.

There are always a few remaining items that require personal attention. Generally I begin with a sink full of hot soapy water, and using a combination of cloths, toothbrushes, and scourers, I carefully wash and clean every item in turn, taking particular care with the items that are used for libations and items that have had bodily contact.

Some items, usually those of primary importance, need special treatment. It is worth taking a detailed look at the proper cleansing techniques for these tools.

We will begin with your wand(s). By now you will be well aware that wands are very special to your Druidic practices. Your wands will be crafted from a variety of woods, fashioned into a variety of forms (rude wands, feathered-tip wands, compound wands, etc.), and finished with a layer of beeswax. It is not difficult, then, to imagine that vigorous, regular washing is soon going to result in the deterioration of the condition of your wands. You must therefore take special precautions with their cleansing.

Use a soft brush dipped in warm, soapy water to gently clean the wand. A midsize paintbrush works well. Brush only in the direction of the grain, that is, from the base of the wand to its tip. When the wand is clean, use a soft, absorbent cloth to dry it. Do not rub the wand with the cloth. Instead, spread the drying cloth over the palm of one hand. Place the base of the wet wand on the cloth, then close the hand holding the cloth, thereby wrapping the cloth around the shaft of the wand. Gently and rhythmically squeeze the cloth in order to help it absorb the dampness from the surface of the wand. Open the hand, slide the wand down so that the next section of its shaft is on the cloth, then close the

hand again and gently squeeze. Repeat the process along the entire length of the shaft until the wand is dry.

The idea behind this method is that by gently squeezing the cloth you are absorbing the moisture on the wand without damaging its surface.

Once the surface is as dry as you can get it with the cloth, place the wand aside, allowing it to slowly dry in the ambient atmosphere. Do not be tempted to put it on a heater or radiator. Accelerating the drying process will nearly always result in distortion, shrinkage, and overdrying of the wood, eventually rendering the wand unusable.

Once the wand is thoroughly dry—and this could take a day or two, depending on the humidity in your area—you will need to give it a new coat of beeswax.

If the wand was involved in bodily contact during the ritual, such as a feathered-tip wand that is used for sexual stimulation, its tip should be dipped in a sterilization solution once it has been cleansed in the usual manner. The wand may then be recoated in beeswax if necessary. This process is described in more detail later in this section.

Remember to cleanse all of your wands on each occasion, not just the ones you have recently used. When they have all been cleansed, place your wands to one side until it is time for the purification ritual.

Your stave will be the next item to tackle. It can be cleaned in the same way as your wands, but it will be necessary for you to invest much more time and effort in the beeswax sealing and polishing. The stave is a much larger and more robust item than the wands, but you will still need to exercise the same caution in the washing and drying process, particularly during the final atmospheric drying. The stave will distort, warp, and split more readily than your wands. Let it dry out completely before you begin applying the beeswax, or else you will seal in the remaining moisture, setting yourself up for problems at a later date.

Apply a series of coats of beeswax to the surface of the stave, buffing each one thoroughly before applying the next. In this way you build up a strong, moisture-proof layer that will protect your stave from the elements during your trips outdoors.

Many people tie adornments and power-giving medallions or icons to the top of their stave in order to enhance its power and protective attributes. This practice has proven effective for many individuals. It is important to remember, however, that these adornments must also be cleansed, as they are capable of harboring all sorts of unpleasant things, particularly if they are organic in origin. Ideally all adornments should be able to be detached from the stave during cleansing, cleaned separately, and then reattached.

Once you are convinced that the stave has been thoroughly cleaned, dried, and resealed, place it to one side to await its purification.

Next turn your attention to your dagger. You will need to apply a little common sense to this particular cleansing, as everyone's dagger is different. Some are simple affairs that can be washed in the same fashion as household cutlery; others are complex, ornate antiques that require special cleaning solutions and agents. Most will fall somewhere in between. What is important is that the dagger blade be clean and sterile (even though it is never to be used as a cutting implement) and that the exterior of the dagger, including its handle and scabbard, be clean and polished.

Once cleansed, the dagger is placed to one side to await the purification ritual.

The remaining items of your cache will usually be those that have seen intimate bodily contact in the sex magic ritual. These include the phallus, fetishes, and any items that have come into contact with or been inserted into the more intimate parts of the body. These items will have been protected by condoms and other protectants, but all the same they carry the highest risk for contamination.

You should have collected these items in a plastic bag or container at the end of your ritual, using sterile gloves to handle them and of course removing and safely disposing of all the condoms that covered them, along with your gloves. Your first task is the thorough washing of each of these objects.

I would strongly recommend that you wash these items in a special plastic bowl designated just for this purpose. Rather than do this in the domestic kitchen, you may choose to take the bowl, filled with hot soapy water, into your workshop, herbarium, or, weather permitting, to a convenient spot outdoors. Add a disinfectant to the soapy water, and wearing sterile gloves, unseal the bag or container and tip the objects into the water. Allow them to soak for a minute or two before beginning to scrub each one vigorously. The washing must be

meticulous. Each item needs to be painstakingly cleaned to the highest possible standard.

Once you have cleaned an item, place it to one side. When all the items are washed, replace the soapy, disinfectant water with fresh clean water and rinse and dry all the items. Don't forget to clean all the phallic items of your cache, whether or not they have been used in your recent ritual.

When your entire collection of ritual tools is clean, you are ready to begin the sterilization of your cache.

There is a wide range of sterilizing preparations available commercially. Some are used in the homebrew process and can be found in homebrew shops. Others are used to sterilize jars and bottles for canning and preserving; these are available from kitchen supply stores. Whatever you choose, make sure it is suitable for use on items that will contain food or drink.

Mix the solution according to the manufacturer's instructions and systematically sterilize every item of your cache according to the instructions on the pack, excluding, of course, the fabric items that you will have laundered earlier. Among the individual items of your cache to be regularly sterilized are your wands, dagger blade and handle, any libation vessels you may use, ladles, spoons, goblets, and anything else that you feel may harbor unwanted bacteria.

Now bring all the items of your cache together in preparation for the purification ritual.

Purifying Your Cache

All the items of your cache are now physically clean and sterile, thanks to the cleansing you have just undertaken. But no matter how well you take care of your tools and equipment, they will inevitably become contaminated by unwanted energies. When this is the case, their individual energy and power will diminish and their ability to act a conduit for channeling your energy and intentions will decline.

You therefore must establish a regular regime of purifying your cache to remove any unwanted contamination and reenergizing the individual items of your cache in order to recover or even increase their potency.

Purifying and energizing are two separate, mystical, magical rituals, and they may or may not be carried out at the same time. If, following their purification, the items of your cache are to be stored until your next working or ritual, you may choose to delay the energizing until the cache is opened again for that ritual. Some individuals argue that the cache is much more potent if it is energized just prior to the ritual, immediately after the pre-ritual cleansing and purification. I agree with this principle, but I still prefer to energize my cache at every opportunity. Therefore I cleanse, purify, and energize my cache before storing it, and I repeat all three stages when I open my cache prior to the ritual or working. This may be considered excessive by some, but I am fastidious about the cleanliness of my ritual tools and would never pass up an opportunity to purify and energize them.

The purification is achieved by anointing each item with compounds representing the four elements. Each compound removes from the object any unwanted or intrusive attribute derived from its own realm.

- Earth is represented by salt, a substance long associated with purification.
- Water is represented by moon-cleansed water fortified with an infusion of purifying herbs.
- Fire is represented by a candle flame or the flame of an oil-burning lamp.
- Air is represented by the smoke of incense made from purifying plants or herbs.

The main preparation for the working is readying these elemental compounds. We will look at each of these in turn.

The salt you use in your workings and occasionally in your rituals must be either mineral or sea salt. Never use table or cooking salt! The Welsh tradition generally uses sea salt, as described in part 1. Store your salt in an airtight canister until you are ready to use it. If you intend to use salt in a particular ritual or working (as in this case), you may wish to place a small amount of your supply in a decorative bowl or vessel before placing it upon your working stone.

To create your purifying water you will need to begin with about a half-pint of moon-cleansed water. The moon-cleansing working is described in part 3. To reinforce the purifying attributes of the water, you will need to steep in it one or

more of the purifying herbs listed below. Depending on the season of your working, you may be able to obtain sprigs of fresh herbs, but a bundle of dried herbs will work just as well. Choose from among the following:

- Bay
- Camphor
- Clove
- Fennel
- Horseradish
- Hyssop
- Juniper
- Lavender
- Nettle
- Parsley
- Peppermint
- Pine
- Rosemary
- Thyme

This list is not exhaustive, but it includes the more commonly available purifying herbs found growing wild in the Celtic nations. There are a small number of flowers also indigenous to the Celtic lands that have similar purifying attributes. The most common of these are the lily and lilac. Float a small bouquet of either or both of these on the surface of your purifying water to further increase its potency.

Place the moon-cleansed water in your cauldron. Some individuals heat the water to assist the infusion. I have found that it has little or no effect on the potency of the infusion, so I always leave the water unheated.

Place your bundle of herb sprigs in the water. If the herbs are fresh, first bruise them lightly in a pestle and mortar to release their natural oils and aromas. Allow the herbs to steep in the water for at least three hours in order for their

HOW THE SEX
MAGIC RITUAL
WORKS

attributes to be absorbed into the liquid. If you wish you can leave the herbs in the water until the purification is complete; they will not harm your working and will continue to fortify your infusion until the last moment.

Purification by fire is best achieved using the flame of a natural wax candle. First place your usual triangle of candles, as described in part 1, at the center of your working stone. In front of them place a row of three or four natural wax candles. This setup allows you to pass each item of your cache along a row of flames, achieving a thorough purification in just one pass.

Alternatively, you can set up a similar row of oil burners, which will produce a similar row of purifying flames. If you choose to use oil burners, augment their fuel oil with a few drops of pine essential oil to further enhance their potency.

To complete the air purification working, you will need to pass each item of your cache through the smoke of burning incense or other natural herbs, spices, woods, and barks. Cedarwood, pine, and clove incense are the most effective for this purpose. If you prefer to use your own harvested ingredients, begin by burning a small piece of charcoal until it glows red and stops smoking. Place it in a fireproof container and place your herbs, spices, woods, or barks on top of it. A plume of scented smoke will rise from the conflagration.

This is the extent of your preparation. Place your container of salt, your vessel of purifying water, your row of candles or oil burners, and your incense burner or charcoal brazier on your working stone along with your cache. You are now ready to begin the working.

The purification, like all other rituals and workings, is carried out inside a Circle, which gives protection to and focuses the power of the Druidic priest or priestess who is facilitating the ritual. Casting and sealing a Circle are described in detail in part 3. For this ritual you will seal the Circle with a triple-knotted rope instead of your dagger, the dagger being, on this occasion, part of the cache that is to be purified.

When your Circle is sealed, you will feel its protective power around you. You may now begin your purification working, taking advantage of the amplified focus and intensified concentration the Circle affords you.

Begin with the earth purification, then proceed through water, fire, and air.

Place all the items of your cache in a semicircle on your working stone (if you have room), on your convocation stone (if you have one present), or on the ground in front of your working stone. Pick up your salt container and sprinkle a little salt onto each tool individually.

The purification ritual works perfectly well without any spoken incantations, but if you wish to chant or speak an incantation you should feel free to do so. Chanting or speaking incantations can help you relax and remove your inhibitions.

This working gives you the ideal opportunity to begin to create your own incantations and chants. Every Druid priest and priestess has his or her own repertoire of chants and incantations; some are spoken out loud, and others are spoken internally. Your personal incantations will closely match your personality, reflect your internal energy, and portray the intentions of your workings. Adopting other people's incantations is both lazy and dangerous. The only power any of your incantations can contain is derived from your own internal energy; if an incantation is not in tune with your internal energy, then it will be powerless or misunderstood. In the case of the latter, it can be dangerous.

Keep the words of your chants and incantations simple. Say exactly what you mean. Make them poetic if you have a gift for language; otherwise, stick to plain language and avoid all those thees and thous I mentioned earlier. Most important, feel comfortable with what you are saying.

You may also want to use music as a background to the ritual. Choose your favorite music or one that matches your mood at the time of the ritual. Relaxing, energizing, mystical, or ambient—the mood of the music should serve your needs. The ambient sounds of wind chimes, dolphin calls, whale songs, and so on, frequently find their way into Druidic ritual.

Continue to sprinkle salt onto each object of your cache until all have received the anointment.

Place aside your salt container and pick up the vessel containing your purification water, together with your feathered-tip wand or sprinkling stick. Sprinkle a little of the purification water onto each of the items in your cache. Again, if you feel it is appropriate, chant or speak your personal incantations as you proceed. When each item has received the water anointment, set aside the water vessel.

Light the row of candles or fuel burners, then pick up each of your ritual objects and pass them through the row of flames. Remember that this is a symbolic act. You do not have to hold each object in the flame long enough to actually sterilize it; instead, simply pass each along the line of flames quickly—very quickly, if the item is flammable. If you feel that any particular object is likely to ignite in the flames or be damaged by the heat, dip it in the purification water vessel to dampen it before passing it through the flames.

When you have completed the flame purification, repeat the process with incense, passing each item through the aromatic smoke. In this case make sure that none of the objects becomes smoke-damaged or stained.

Continue chanting or speaking your incantations throughout the ritual if you feel comfortable doing so.

You have now completed the purification working and your cache is ready to be stored. If you prefer, you may pack your cache into its storage containers or bags within the protection of the Circle. But before you can take your cache outside the Circle, you must first unseal and erase your Circle.

To unseal and open the entry portal to your Circle, lift the triple-knotted rope from its position at the portal, saying:

"The work is done, the Circle is opened."

Untie all three knots. With the rope once again held in the hands of your outstretched arms, walk to the vessel containing the purification water, dip one loose end of the rope into the water, and say:

"And so it ends."

You may now set the rope aside, as the Circle has been opened and the working is at an end.

The process of erasing the Circle is explained in detail in part 3.

You may now assemble all the items of your cache together and take them to their storage place.

CLEANSING
AND PURIFYING
YOUR CACHE

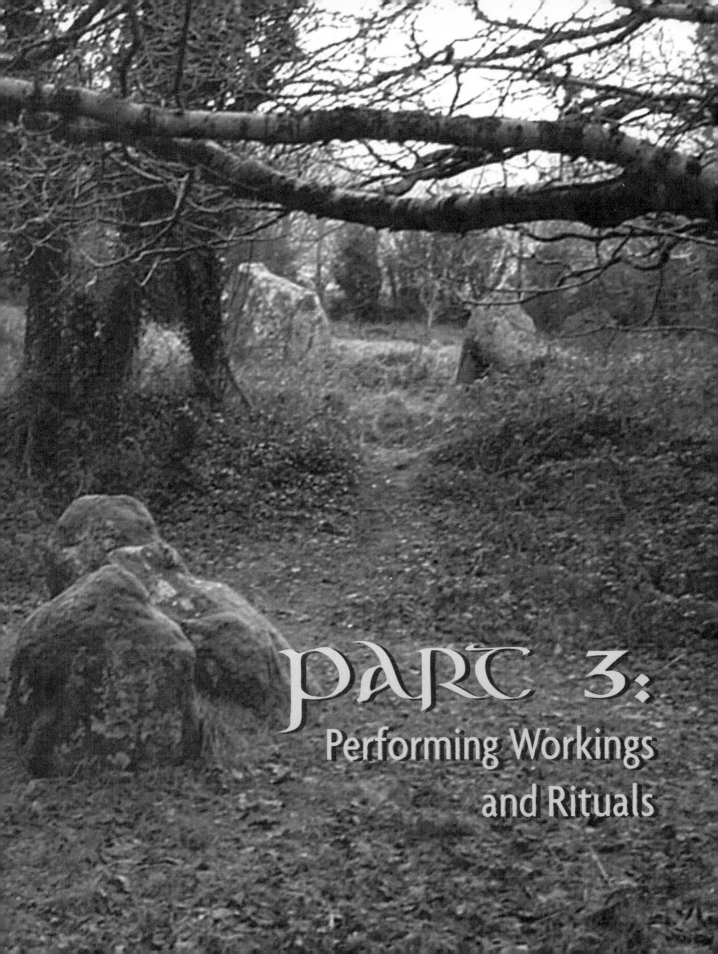

PART 3:
Performing Workings and Rituals

The Intention

Before you begin your association with the workings and rituals in this section, it is essential that you fully understand and appreciate the intention of your involvement.

Some modern-day Druidic organizations and practitioners seem to have completely lost the fundamental concepts of the belief system related to Druidism and its simple pagan origins. In addition, a number of aspects of contemporary Druidism are both confusing and misleading. These difficulties and contradictions do not exist in the tradition that I was taught, and I find it difficult to understand the rationale behind their introduction.

I am particularly troubled by the ideas of intercession and deities in some forms of contemporary Druidism. By this I mean the idea of using saintlike individuals from historic references to act on behalf of worshipers and the elevation of some of the more famous traditional folk heroes to modern-day deities.

As a young man I followed the same progression through the tradition as generations of young men and women had done before me. I was introduced to Druidism in a very subtle way. It was so subtle, in fact, that I was totally unaware that I was being prepared for my later initiation and that I was being given important knowledge that later allowed me to make the conscious, informed choice to continue my progress in the Druidic tradition in my adult life.

As I have explained earlier, many of the more complex philosophical issues related to Druidic tradition are initially taught as parables. Over the years many of these parables have found their way into the complicated folklore of the Celtic nations.

Parables, as you know, are easily understood stories that explain, usually by examples the learner can relate to, a much more complex philosophy. Parables need not be factual stories; they seldom are. They need not contain the absolute truth; in fact, many contain very far-fetched accounts given by extremely unbelievable individuals. All the same, they serve a very valuable purpose and have done so throughout history.

In the case of the early Celts and the emerging Druidic tradition, parables served to explain the unrecorded history of the arrival of the Celts in Wales, Ireland, Scotland, and the other Celtic settlements, together with advanced principles of cosmic importance. Through simple, easily understood stories they provided a vivid account of history, social behavior, clan structure, a creation myth, and much more, to an unsophisticated and uneducated populace. In many cases, the teachers themselves had only a superficial understanding of the concepts their parables attempted to explain. After all, even now, with all our cutting-edge technologies and advanced scientific theories, we understand only a small percentage of what is actually going on in the cosmos of our own existence.

The parables grew as the need to explore and explain more and more of the principles of our existence burgeoned. Many of the parables spilled over into the realm of song and folklore. As they did, their principal characters became heroes among the Celts. Their status grew and grew as the stories of their adventures became more and more exaggerated. Their exploits became more and more fanciful and eventually entered the mystical world of magic. The only possible explanation for their superhuman and supernatural exploits was that they possessed or could control forces that were beyond the reach of other mere mortals. By the time the tales were written into history, much of their origin was lost or misunderstood.

When these historic writings were revisited during the Romantic period, the idea of a pantheon of Celtic hero gods was very appealing, and so with no further ado they were elevated to their present-day status. Since that moment on, generations of well-meaning academics and poorly taught "Druids" have perpetuated and developed the idea of unique Druidic gods. Some appear to be related to Nordic tradition, others are taken from Roman deities, and still others derive from a wide range of pagan gods. The truth is that none of them have any validity whatsoever in the Druidic tradition.

You may ask, "With what authority can you make these claims?" Well, as every true Druid will know, the explanation of this distorted history is itself part

of the early stages of the training of young initiates in the tradition. I was taught it myself as a child.

Druidic tradition is based on a belief in the collective energy and its all-encompassing authority. There are no deities or intercessors that stand between the individual and his or her ability to influence the collective energy. Druidism accepts the deities of all religions while acknowledging the existence of none. Druids offer up no prayers to any gods; the words used in Druidic workings and rituals are a means of channeling and focusing energy. The collective energy cannot be influenced by words; words are simply a means of human communication, and they have no effect outside that sphere. The power of every spell and intention comes from the generated energy of those who cast and bind it, not from the words that are spoken.

No one, not even a Druidic priest or priestess, can intercede on your behalf, as only you know the true intention of your spell. A priest or priestess may facilitate a group generation of energy; he or she may add personal energy to that generated by the Gathering. But it is for you and you alone to compose your spell in such a way that it encapsulates your true intention.

So do not waste your time and effort praying to the pagan gods or the supposed Celtic deities. Both the gods and the idea of prayer are an anathema to the Druidic tradition.

Do not allow yourself to be confused with mention of gods, prayers, saints, or any other form of misguided wisdom. Your workings, your rituals, and the words you speak during them are a means of focusing and fortifying your internal energy. Sex magic is not a religious ritual but a means of amplifying and projecting that energy, nurturing it on its journey to its recipients, and binding it to them. In this way your spell can influence individuals, groups, or even the collective energy itself. Focus only on your own intention; develop your strength of will.

Once you have clarified your intentions, you may then focus your attention on the workings and rituals that follow.

PERFORMING

WORKINGS

AND RITUALS

Personal Preparation

The first step in every Druidic activity is personal preparation: preparing your body, internal energy, and mind for the task ahead. This is a three-stage task. The first step, cleansing the body, is usually carried out at home prior to the working or ritual. The second step, cleansing the internal energy, can be carried out either at home or at the place of the working or ritual, depending on the extent of cleansing the individual feels is required. The third step, preparing the mind, must be carried out in the moments just before the working or ritual begins, therefore it is inevitably undertaken at the site of the working or ritual.

Cleansing the Body

As a matter of hygiene, your body must be physically clean before a working or ritual, as you will most likely be coming into direct bodily contact with others. How you clean your body is determined by:

- The level of internal energy you feel in your body

- Whether you are cleansing yourself or another person is undertaking the task

- The amount of time you can dedicate to the task

If you feel your internal energy is at low ebb or if you feel listless, take this opportunity to regenerate some of that energy.

One quick and effective rejuvenative cleansing technique is the cool shower. Most people will find this invigorating and stimulating.

A less shocking method is to take an herbal bath. There is a range of herbal bath products available commercially. Alternatively, you can place a few drops of an appropriate essential oil in your bath water or, as I prefer, allow a few sprigs of fresh herbs to infuse the bath water. This is a centuries-old, worldwide practice, only recently made popular in the West by the development of aromatherapy.

Herbs to choose from for an energizing herbal bath are:

- Cinnamon

- Marigold

- Peppermint

- Myrrh

- Primrose

- Thyme

If, on the other hand, you feel your internal energy is overactive and you are overly stressed, you will need to relax in a stress-relieving herbal bath. The best herbs for this purpose are:

- Bay

- Clove

- Lavender

- Juniper

- Rosemary

If you are using fresh herbs, tie them together into a bundle, bruise them a little to encourage the release of their natural oils, and place them in the warm bath water at least ten minutes before you bathe to give them the opportunity to release their fragrance and attributes.

Use a gentle, natural soap for your cleansing, and once you have cleansed your entire body, lie back and enjoy the aromatic water. You will feel the stress flow from your body and your energy increase as it absorbs the attributes of the herbs.

It's also a good idea to burn a little incense in the room as you bathe. Try cinnamon for energizing or cedarwood for relaxation. Turn off the lights, light a few candles, and play some ambient music to create an even more relaxing environment.

Whichever atmosphere you decide to create, you will emerge from your bath with a clean and fragrant body, a new sense of purpose, and a stabilized internal energy.

Some fundamentalist Druids will cleanse only in rainwater, ideally only as it falls from the sky. This a wonderful experience but can be hard to arrange. Few things lend such a sense of communion with nature and the collective energy as standing naked in the rain and cleansing yourself with natural soap and bunches of fragrant herbs.

Having someone cleanse your body for you can be a most exhilarating experience too. Mutual cleansing is yet another option.

Try to dedicate as much time as is feasible to your bodily cleansing session. It can be a time of great creativity, and I often experience it as a time when I find solutions to many of the problems that confront me. The modern world does not present us with too many opportunities to lie back and contemplate our circumstances, so don't allow the opportunities to slip through your fingers on the few occasions that they occur.

When proceeding immediately from the cleansing to the working or ritual, some people choose to dress in a simple form of ceremonial garb. The choice is yours, but bear in mind that if you are traveling across town to the site of your ritual, it may be embarrassing if you are stopped for a traffic violation or have to leave your car for some other reason when you are dressed in some form of extravagant regalia. Actually, it would be even more embarrassing if you were stopped in the traditional Druidic ritual garb of absolutely no clothes at all! As a compromise, I suggest wearing loose-fitting, sensible clothing until you are at the site and ready to begin your ritual.

Purifying Internal Energy

You have already attended to some of the needs of your internal energy as you bathed and cleansed your body. The efforts you have made so far have served to stabilize your internal energy in preparation for the more concentrated cleansing you are about to undertake. At this stage your internal energy is neutral—not torpid, overenergized, or erratic.

Purifying your internal energy frees it from any extraneous or intrusive influences. This may be achieved through the same tranquil meditation process described in part 1. The effect of your meditative purification may be enhanced by the use of sympathetic essential oils, incense, and herbs. These may be burned or evaporated, allowing their attributes to permeate your consciousness. I recommend the following:

- Bay
- Bladderwrack
- Borage
- Cinnamon
- Camphor
- Cloves
- Dandelion
- Lavender
- Mace
- Marigold
- Rose
- Sage
- Thyme

All of these will benefit your psychic powers and focus your concentration on the purification.

If the purification is taking place immediately prior to the sex magic ritual, make sure your selection contains cinnamon or lavender, as they contain particularly potent sex magic attributes.

To begin the purification, seat yourself comfortably in your usual meditation environment. You may now choose either to make the visualized journey to one of the special places you have reserved within the collective energy especially for meditation or to begin your purification exactly where you are.

The first step is to focus on your awareness of your own internal energy. Again, this takes practice. Being able to turn your consciousness inward and explore

what is happening within your "self" is a difficult concept. I was taught a visualization technique to help me understand this exceptionally valuable ability.

Once you are settled and tranquil, visualize your "mind" or "self" as a glade of trees, a forest clearing with many paths and tracks radiating from it. For a moment, travel outside your body and see yourself sitting in that clearing. Make yourself familiar with the trees that enclose it and the paths that radiate from it. Look for a particularly wide path that distinguishes itself from the others by its width and the high trees that border it. Stand before this path and look down along it. It appears to be endless, stretching off into infinity. Remember where this path is within the clearing; you will soon be using it.

Behind these trees and down along these paths are all the prospective disruptive and intrusive energies that are likely to inhibit your internal energy's effective workings. Return to your body and sit quietly, waiting for the first of them to appear.

As your consciousness presents each of these energies to you, confront it, deal with it in the best way possible, and send it down the wide path to infinity.

Once a particular disruptive energy has been dispatched, it may never trouble you again, but it also may return time and time again to confront you. Whichever is the case, it has, for the time being, been dispatched from your consciousness at least for the next few hours while you participate in your ritual.

As each successive disruptive energy is removed from your internal energy, you will begin to feel lighter and less troubled, and a sense of well-being will begin to settle over your consciousness. Eventually the procession of disruptive energies will slow down and finally stop. When it seems that there are no more to deal with, make a visualized journey to each of the paths and tracks, call down them, and search them for any remaining disruptive energies, no matter how small.

Once you are confident that all have been dealt with, visualize yourself sealing the entrance to the wide path with a dagger or triple-knotted rope in the same manner that you seal your cast Circle. This prevents the disruptive energies from reentering your consciousness or interfering with your internal energy.

As you return to worldly awareness from your meditative state, you will be bathed in a confident glow of well-being.

PERSONAL
PREPARATION

By definition, a disruptive energy is any form of energy that interferes with or disrupts your personal internal energy. If it is an external energy, such as a magnetic force, a ley line, a noise, a light, or something else in your environment, it can be dealt with in the physical world. A ley line is a narrow, invisible line of energy that runs across the landscape below the surface of the earth. Undetectable to the known human senses, ley lines may be discovered by dowsing in the same way as subterranean water. These lines, which are said to be two or three feet wide, are reputed to have a subtle effect on the human psyche. As a result, people have been inspired from the beginning of time to erect places of worship or profound spiritual awareness along the lay of these lines. Places like Stonehenge, Glastonbury, and many other major religious buildings and sites in the U.K. are reputed by some to be connected by these invisible lines of force and energy.

Ley lines are not to be confused with earth currents, which consist of a worldwide system of eight loops of electric currents distributed on both sides of the equator, together with a series of smaller loops near the poles. This system is detectable by the use of scientific measuring instruments, and there is no suggestion that ley lines form part of this complex network of currents. Just like ley lines, however, earth currents also have the potential to interfere with or disrupt your personal energy.

If you are being disturbed by a magnetic force or disrupted by any other external energy, find it, eliminate it, or move location.

On the other hand, disruptive energies may also be internal. These internal disruptive forces include stress, worry, preoccupations, memories, plans, and so on; they are any part of your conscious awareness that interferes with or intrudes upon your internal energy and disrupts its ability to focus. It is these worries, memories, and preoccupations that are dealt with in the course of your purification.

If your purification is carried out well before your ritual or working, be prepared to have to maintain your purified state until your ritual begins. It may be very difficult to remove yourself from any internal or external influences that negate your purification if in the meantime you have to function in the everyday world for any length of time. My advice is not to begin the purification until you are preparing for your ritual. I find that the best time for purification is immediately after the cleansing and just before I leave for the site of the ritual.

Mental Preparation and Awareness

This is the final stage of preparation prior to the ritual or working itself, and it must be carried out in the moments just before you cast the Circle.

When your body has been cleansed, your internal energy has been purified, and your ritual space has been laid out in preparation for your working, then is the time to begin your mental preparation. You find yourself standing before the ritual space, possibly clad in your ceremonial garb, with your Gathering milling around you. You now need to prepare yourself mentally for the task ahead and raise your awareness of what is going on around and within you to a higher level. You should have your stave with you.

To begin your mental preparation, place your feet together and the base of your stave on the ground between them, with its tip pointing skyward. Holding the shaft of your stave with both hands at shoulder height, push the stave away from your body until your arms are fully extended, so that your body and the stave form an inverted pyramid. The point of the pyramid is formed by the conjunction of your two feet and the base of the stave; the triangular base of the pyramid is described by the lines formed between your first shoulder and the stave, between the stave and your second shoulder, and between your two shoulders.

The focus of power in all pyramids is the central point of the base. The converging sides serve to focus and concentrate this energy before it is projected from the point or tip. The purpose of your inverted triangular pyramid is to focus your internal energy downward, toward the earth from where the matter of which you are formed originates.

Now you want to position the core of your mental preparation and awareness (your mind) at the center point of power within the pyramid (the center of the triangular base). To do this, simply drop your head forward and look at the convergent point at your feet. You will find that your head is in exactly the place you want.

This stance is used frequently in a range of ritual acts because it focuses, concentrates, and projects your energies and thoughts toward the earth, one of the principal recipients of spells and intentions.

In this position you will instantly feel the power of your internal energy. Systematically banish all unwanted and unnecessary thoughts from your

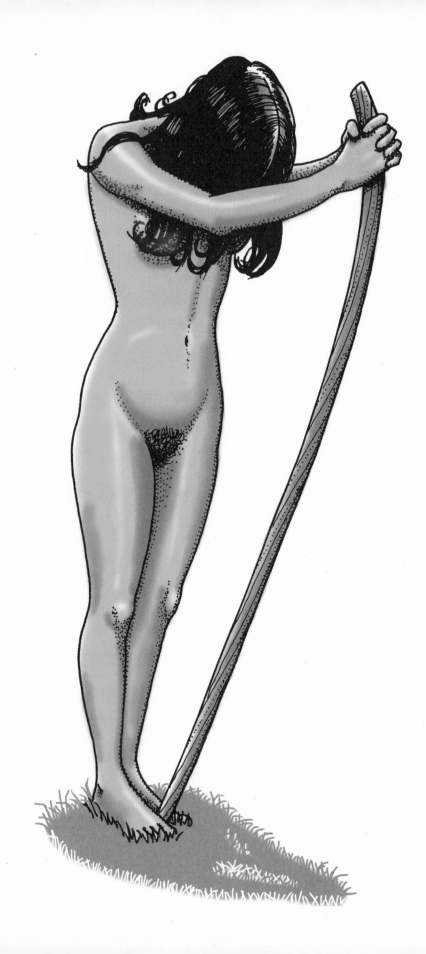

consciousness and replace them with positive thoughts related to the ritual you are about to facilitate. Briefly go through the planned successions of the ritual, placing them in order and organizing your intended actions accordingly.

Once you have mentally mapped out your plan for the ritual, focus your concentration on raising your mental and physical awareness. I use five simultaneous actions to do this. If you plan to emulate my method, you will have to remember to place a few leaves of peppermint or spearmint in your mouth before you take up the inverted pyramid stance. Keep them at the side of your mouth, and do not chew them until the appropriate moment.

You will introduce each action in turn, maintaining the previous ones as you go so that as you arrive at the fifth, all five actions will be working concurrently.

Focus first on the sense of feeling in your hands. Rub your hands slightly against the shaft of the stave that you are holding. Concentrate on feeling the sensory stimulation of touch. Now squeeze the stave shaft in a pulsating fashion, feeling the pressure on your hands. Continue this rubbing and pulsing as you proceed.

Now focus on your sense of sight. Examine the ground upon which you are standing. Do not turn your head, but look intensively at the small area surrounding your feet. Try and take in as much detail as you can. Look at every speck of dust, every grain of dirt; try to absorb the infinite details of the area you are scrutinizing. Add this to the previous action and maintain them both.

Next focus on the sense of taste. Begin rhythmically chewing the mint leaves you have in your mouth. Focus on the release of the flavors from the leaves. Experience the taste in all areas of your mouth—the whole surface of your tongue, underneath your tongue, at the roof of your mouth, at the back of your mouth. Let the experience fill your mouth as you chew. Add this sensory experience to your vision and touch actions and keep all three going at the same time.

By now you should begin to feel a sense of heightened awareness throughout your whole body and mind, a feeling of increased energy and amplified sensory activity.

A priestess in the inverted pyramid stance. The energy is projected to the center of the base of the inverted pyramid where the priestess has positioned her head.

PERSONAL
PREPARATION

155

Next focus on the sense of smell. As you chew the mint leaves they release both flavor and fragrance. Focus now on their fragrance. You will be able to smell their perfume as you breathe out through your mouth and in through your nose. You will also sense their fragrance migrating through the areas that connect your mouth with your nasal passages. Feel the aroma acting on all of your nasal sensors, filling your head with their perfume. You are now stimulating four of your senses simultaneously.

Finally, focus on your sense of hearing. As you chew your mint leaves, begin to hum or chant softly and quietly. Listen to the sound of your voice, hearing it resonate through your body as well as the air.

Now try and make yourself aware of all five senses at once. You know that each is being stimulated by a source under your control, so if you are "missing" one from the group, amplify its source a little: squeeze harder, chew faster, or hum louder. Think of each sense as a channel on your stereo that can be amplified or reduced to bring the overall experience into balance.

Once you have balanced your sensory perception, experience it for a few moments, feeling the excitement and letting it build to a crescendo before returning to the conscious world again.

Your senses will now be raised and tuned and your awareness heightened; you will have an acute sensory awareness of the world around you. In this uniquely lucid state you are now fully prepared for the ritual or working you are about to undertake.

Casting the Circle

Every Druidic ritual is conducted within a protective Circle, and the drawing or casting of this protective Circle is one of the most significant responsibilities of the Druidic priest or priestess. The purpose of the Circle is to protect those participants within it from any potentially intrusive or harmful energies on the outside, to focus the energies of the participants on the ritual, and to contain the Gathering's generated energy until the time of projection, preventing it from dispersing. It also denotes the boundaries of the ritual activities; those within are included, and those outside are not.

There are a number of ways to cast a Circle. We shall concentrate on just one of these, the triple-cast Circle, as it best suits the sex magic ritual. It is also the strongest form of the cast Circles and offers the greatest protection to those inside it.

As the name suggests, the triple-cast Circle is cast three times, each time using the attributes of one of the basic elements, air, water, and fire. The fourth basic element is the earth upon which the Circle is cast, so once the Circle is complete, its occupants have the attributes of all four basic elements for their protection.

The word "circle" is slightly misleading. Druidic lore, being fundamentally based in nature, is not very keen on symmetry. The Circle is never really a perfect one. More often it is a line connecting the bases of a ring of trees or a crudely drawn approximation of a circle. It would never be drawn in a perfect geometric fashion as achieved when using a central peg and a length of string to describe the circumference.

The principles governing the casting of a Circle are as follows:

- It is always cast from the inside.

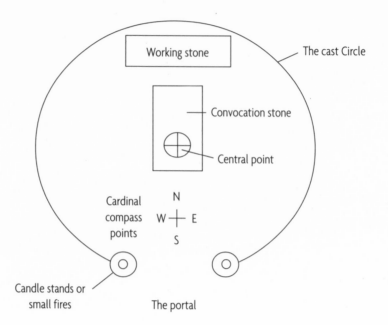

Working stone

The cast Circle

Convocation stone

Central point

Cardinal compass points

N
W ┼ E
S

Candle stands or small fires

The portal

- Although never a precise circle, it must not have any sharp curves or corners.

- The Circle must always present a visible boundary for the participants of the Gathering to respect.

- The Circle will always have a center point marker and a marker indicating the cardinal points of the compass.

- The working stone will always be located at the northern cardinal point of the Circle and lie in the west/east orientation.

- The convocation stone will always be in a south/north orientation, with the center point of the Circle falling on the surface of the convocation stone just where the head of the Principal Conduit will lie.

- The Circle will always have an entrance portal in its circumference, with candles or small fires at each side of the portal. The portal will always be in the southern side of the circumference so that as the participants enter they are facing north, toward the working stone.

- The Circle will be of a size to accommodate the number of the Gathering.

Other than these basic factors the Circle may take whatever form the person casting it wishes.

PERFORMING
WORKINGS
AND RITUALS

Casting the protective Circle using the stave. Note the way in which the stave is held, as this is the traditional method and has major significance. The priestess is walking in a clockwise direction casting the Circle from one entry portal to the other. The stave is held approximately 3 inches from the ground.

The Triple-Cast Circle: The Ritual

Choosing the site for your ritual should be one of your very first considerations. You will need to define first the purpose of the ritual, then exactly how the ritual is to be facilitated.

Some of the factors that affect the choice of site will be:

- The number of participants at the Gathering
- The site's accessibility
- Whether the site needs to be indoors or outside

- The weather
- Whether the ritual will be held at night or during the day
- What ritual tools and accessories will be required and how they will be transported and placed within the site

There are other factors to take into account, of course. The response of your internal energy to the location you are contemplating is immensely important. The influences of local ley lines and other external influences will also have to be considered.

Many ancient pre-Christian gathering sites have particularly potent intrinsic energies that have been amplified by the resonance of the rituals that were conducted on them for millennia. If you are not able to find or use one of these energized locations, the next best choice should be a neutral location, a site that is free from negative influences. This is often the case if you are intending to facilitate an indoor ritual. There will be very few positively energized indoor sites, but unless you are unfortunate enough to select an indoor location that has at some time been contaminated by previous workings of a negative influence, you will be beginning with a neutral environment.

It will be necessary for you to cleanse and purify the site as explained earlier to safeguard against any lingering unwanted influences. Cleansing a ritual site is the physical cleaning of the site prior to use—sweeping, dusting, washing, whatever is required to make the site usable. Purifying is the removal of unwanted energies and influences, achieved by anointing the site with the four elements, employing the same technique as used in purifying the cache (see part 2). Once your site is selected and you have gathered together the tools and accessories for your working, you may begin to arrange your ritual site.

The first step in casting any Circle is to identify the orientation of your ritual site. This is normally done by using an ordinary compass. There are, however, some people who have the gift of being able to dowse the cardinal points; others choose to use the traditional Druid's stone or a magnetized needle.

Whatever method you choose, once you have oriented your site, mark the cardinal points on the ground. This can be done with a simple cross somewhere near the proposed entry portal of the Circle showing the four cardinal points of

the compass. Then walk to the "notional" center of the Circle and mark the center point with a similar cross, again oriented to the cardinal points.

Depending on your chosen location, you may now need to erect your portable working stone and convocation stone, if that is what you are using, and set out your ritual tools and candles before casting the Circle. Remember that the head of the person lying on the convocation stone must be located at the center point of the Circle. The person will be lying in the north/south orientation, feet pointing toward the working stone and head at the center. Once the stones are erected and your ritual tools are in place, you may begin the working for casting a triple-cast Circle.

For this working you will need:

- **Your stave.** To cast the first Circle.

- **Your salt canister.** Should contain enough salt to cast the second Circle.

- **A flask of moon-cleansed water.** To anoint the Circle.

- **Two floor-standing candleholders plus two natural wax candles, or enough material to set two small fires.** These will be set on each side of the entry portal of the Circle and will be used to cast the third Circle.

To begin the working, stand at the southern extremity of the proposed Circle, at the center point of the proposed entry portal, facing the north and the center mark of your intended Circle. Place a candleholder at your left and right sides, arms' width apart. This marks the entry portal.

Like most other rituals and workings facilitated by a Druidic priest or priestess, the Circle-casting working begins with the priest or priestess focusing their sensory awareness using the power position of the inverted triangular pyramid. Standing between the entry portal candles, assume the inverted pyramid stance and focus your awareness as explained earlier. Once you are confident that you have achieved your desired level of sensory awareness, lift your stave in both hands as high into the air as possible and say:

"I begin the casting and call upon the energy of the elements to protect all those within."

Then place the base of your stave at the base of the candleholder on your

left. Step inward into the inside of the circumference and begin to draw or cast the Circle on the ground, encompassing the area you plan to use in your ritual. You will end at the base of the second candleholder, thereby completing an unbroken circle from one candleholder to the other, leaving only the space between them as the portal.

Set your stave aside by leaning it against your working stone. (As a point of etiquette you should never lay your stave flat on the ground.) Pick up your salt canister from the working stone, open it, and, holding it high in the air with both hands, say:

"I continue the casting and call upon the energy of the elements to protect all those within."

Beginning at the same point at the base of the candleholder on your left, walk around the inner circumference of your Circle sprinkling salt on the ground at the Circle's perimeter until you again reach the second candleholder, thereby casting an unbroken salt Circle from one candleholder to the other.

Replace the salt canister upon the working stone and pick up your flask of moon-cleansed water. Begin your casting again at the base of the candleholder on the left-hand side of the entrance portal, only this time as you progress around the Circle to the second candleholder, sprinkle or pour a trail of moon-cleansed water onto the perimeter. As you do this say:

"I continue the casting and again call upon the energy of the elements to protect all those within."

Replace the flask of moon-cleansed water onto the working stone and pick up your matches or flint or whatever you intend to use to ignite your candles. Walk to the first candleholder and light its candle. Remove the second candle (from the candleholder on the right) from its holder and light it from the flame of the first candle. Holding the second candle high in the air with both hands, say:

"I complete the casting and call upon the energy of the elements to protect all those within."

Place the wick of the second candleholder back into the flame of the first candleholder, and from that point walk the perimeter of the cast Circle with the

flame of the second candle directly over the previously cast circumference. When you arrive at the second candleholder, place the lit candle in it, thereby having cast an unbroken flame Circle from the first candleholder to the second. As you place the candle into the candleholder, say:

"The casting is complete, the Circle is closed. Once sealed, let none defile its protection."

This then completes the Circle casting. The Circle should now be entered and exited only through the portal left between the two candleholders.

Sealing the Circle: The Ritual

The triple-cast Circle is the most powerful protective Circle you can cast. There is little point in casting such a powerful protective Circle, however, if you leave its portal vulnerable. You must then triple-seal your Circle to maintain its integrity.

The Circle is sealed only once all the participants are inside its boundaries and the ritual or working is about to proceed.

Circles may be sealed with a dagger or, less often, with a triple-knotted rope. The triple-knotted rope is usually used only if the dagger is required for some other purpose during the ritual. In the case of the triple-cast Circle, some people feel that the affinity of the triple casting and the triple knot gives the Circle a stronger protective quality. I understand this argument but feel that as the dagger sealing is a triple-action sealing, with the dagger being opened and closed three times, it has just as strong an affinity as the triple-knotted rope.

The triple-cast Circle is sealed as follows. You will need:

- **Your dagger.** Used to seal the Circle.
- **A cauldron containing moon-cleansed water.** To anoint your dagger.
- **Your salt canister.** Should contain enough salt to seal the portal.
- **A natural wax candle.** Its flame will seal the portal.

Having cast the triple-cast Circle, pick up the dagger.

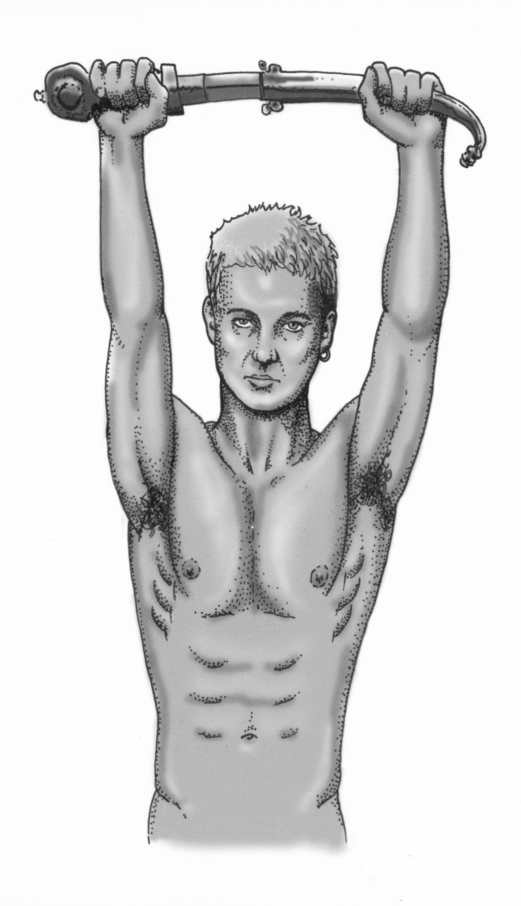

Stand before your working stone. Holding the dagger above your head with the handle in the right hand and its scabbard in your left (reverse these instructions if you are left-handed), draw the dagger from its scabbard. Dip the tip of the dagger into the cauldron of moon-cleansed water, at the same time saying:

"And so it begins."

Standing before the working stone (thereby facing north), place the dagger approximately halfway into its scabbard. Hold the partly sheathed dagger high in the air and say:

"I am part of the collective energy, I hold its power within me, as does every other creation. I use my being to empower this dagger and awaken the potential energy within it."

Slam the dagger fully into its scabbard with enough force to let the participants in the Gathering know that you have done it.

Turn ninety degrees to the right (so that you are now facing the east). Holding the dagger high in the air as before, half-draw the dagger from its scabbard and say:

"With this dagger I begin the seal, and I call upon all unsympathetic energies to leave this Circle."

Slam the dagger closed again.

Turn one hundred and eighty degrees (so that you are now facing west). Holding the dagger high in the air as before, half-draw the dagger from its scabbard and say:

"With this dagger I strengthen the seal and ask a second time for all unsympathetic energies to leave this Circle."

Slam the dagger closed again.

Turn ninety degrees to your left (so that you are now facing south). Holding the dagger high in the air as before, half-draw the dagger from its scabbard and say:

"With this dagger I make the seal and ask a third time for all unsympathetic energies to leave this Circle."

A young initiate Druid beginning the ritual by unsheathing the dagger and invoking its potential energies.

Slam the dagger closed again.

Facing the south (as you now stand), you are also facing the entrance portal to the Circle. Walk to the entrance portal and place the fully sheathed dagger on the floor between the entry pillars. As you do this say:

"With this dagger I seal this Circle. I invoke its protection. I focus my energy within it. Let all those without stay without."

This ends the first sealing.

Now pick up your salt canister, walk back to the portal, and sprinkle a line of salt from the base of the left candleholder to the base of the right candleholder. As you do this say:

"With this salt I double-seal this Circle. I invoke its protection. I focus my energy within it. Let all those without stay without."

This ends the second sealing.

Replace the salt canister on the working stone and pick up the natural wax candle. Walk back to the portal and light the candle from the flame of the left-hand portal candle. Move the hand-held candle slowly from the left-hand side of the portal to the right. As you do this say:

"With this flame I triple-seal this Circle. I invoke its protection. I focus my energy within it. Let all those without stay without."

Blow out the candle and place it next to the dagger on the ground between the portal candles.

This ends the third and final sealing.

Your Circle is now sealed. You will feel its protective power around you and experience the focus and concentration it affords you.

If you choose to use the triple-knotted rope seal, you will need a length of rope about two meters long. Mark the center point of the rope and place it on the working stone before you begin the ritual.

The Circle is sealed as follows.

Having cast the circle, pick up the rope.

Holding the rope stretched between your outstretched hands, dip one of the hanging ends into the cauldron of purifying water. At the same time speak the opening statement:

"And so it begins."

Standing before the working stone (thereby facing north), hold the stretched rope high in the air and say:

"I am part of the collective energy, I hold its power within me, as does every other creation. I use my being to empower this rope and awaken the potential energy within it."

Turn ninety degrees to the right (so that you are now facing east). Lower the rope and tie the first knot about 8 inches to the right of the center point. As you do this, say:

"With this first knot I begin the seal, and I call upon all unsympathetic energies to leave this Circle."

When you have tied the first knot, turn one hundred and eighty degrees (so that you are now facing west). Tie the second knot at the center mark on the rope. As you do this, say:

"With this second knot I strengthen the seal and ask a second time for all unsympathetic energies to leave this Circle."

Having tied the second knot, turn ninety degrees to your left (so that you are now facing south). Tie the third knot about 8 inches to the left of the center point of the rope. As you do so, say:

"With this third knot I make the seal and ask a third time for all unsympathetic energies to leave this Circle."

By facing south, you are also facing the entrance portal to the Circle. Walk to the entrance portal and place the extended rope on the floor between the entry pillars. As you do this, say:

"I seal this Circle. I invoke its protection. I focus my energy within it. Let all those without stay without."

The triple-knotted rope may be used as an alternative to the dagger to seal the protective Circle.

Sealing the Circle is an imperative part of every ritual or working. It should be done with the utmost care and consideration. It is the final act leading up to the ritual and also the last solitary act by the priest or priestess prior to the group activity of the ritual. If it is done correctly and with power, it imbues a sense of security and intensifies the focus of the Gathering. If it is done lethargically, it will not have the same effect.

Unsealing and Erasing the Circle: The Ritual

At the end of each ritual or working the protective Circle is unsealed, and once all the participants of the Gathering have left the Circle it is erased. Never leave a cast Circle standing until the next ritual; this simply does not work. Even if you are using a permanent site such as a standing stone Circle, as I often do, it is essential that the protective Circle be cast and erased for every individual ritual or working.

Make it your habit to unseal the protective Circle as soon as the ritual is over. Do not stand around talking to the other participants, and do not allow them to stand around talking to each other inside the sealed Circle. Make the unsealing of the Circle a part of the ritual; until the Circle is unsealed, the ritual is not over. Educate your Gathering to stay focused and involved until the final words, "It is ended," are spoken.

To unseal a triple-sealed Circle, first pick up the hand-held candle from its place on the ground between the portal candles. Relight the candle from the flame of the right-hand candle, then move the flame of the hand-held candle slowly across the portal to the flame of the left-hand candle. Hold the lit candle high in the air and say:

"I remove the flame seal."

Blow out the hand-held candle and return it to the working stone.

Return to the portal. With your right hand disperse the salt line on the ground between the portal candles, saying:

"I remove the salt seal."

Next pick up the dagger from the ground. Holding it high in the air, remove the dagger from its scabbard and say:

"The seal is broken, the Circle is open."

Walk to the cauldron on the working stone; dip the tip of the dagger into the moon-cleansed water within it, saying:

"And so it ends."

Replace the dagger in its scabbard and place it on the working stone.

Turn to face the Gathering. Lift your hands high in the air for all to see and say in a loud voice:

"It has ended!"

This ends the ritual and indicates to the Gathering that they may now disperse, leaving the Circle collect their clothing and dress.

Harvesting, Cleansing, and Energizing Your Wand(s) and Stave

We have already seen that your wand(s) and stave are your most powerful and cherished Druidic tools. None of your other tools are quite as important in channeling and influencing energies.

Because of their unique status, the cleansing, purification, and energizing of newly harvested wands and staves is a very important working. Bearing in mind that you will keep and use some of these tools as your most useful and potent instruments for the remainder of your life, it is easy to understand why they demand such special consideration.

Note: The general cleansing and purification of mature wands and staves can be undertaken as described in part 2. The workings that follow concern newly harvested wands and staves only. I will focus on wands; staves are harvested, cleansed, and energized in exactly the same manner as wands.

Protective Circles are always cast with a stave. If the workings are for your very first stave, however, you may use your dagger to cast the protective Circle.

Harvesting: The Working

As you will remember from part 1, there are a number of essential principles that need to be adhered to when harvesting wands. The choice of the donor tree is the foremost consideration, followed closely by the time of harvesting, whether by sunlight or moonlight. These considerations determine the innate characteristics of your wand and dictate the types of uses it will be put to. What follows is more concerned with the potency of your wand, its power to channel energy and transmit its attributes, and not the character of the attributes it possesses.

Once you have decided what attributes your new wand needs to possess and have identified the type of wood you feel most reflects that choice, then you must begin your search for your donor tree. For me this usually entails long forest walks, lakeside visits, and rummaging among the local woodland for possible candidates. I try to select at least two potential donor trees and revisit them many times before finally deciding which to work with.

Look for a healthy, mature tree, ideally one growing within a group of trees of the same species. Your intention should always be to minimize the damage to the tree and its environment. If you select a healthy tree from a community of trees of the same species, the impact of harvesting is minimal.

You will always harvest your branch from the north side of the tree trunk. You can determine which is the north side of the tree by using a cheap walker's compass. Select a branch that grows on the north side of the tree's trunk with its tip pointing directly toward the north, so that it is aligned in a south/north orientation. These branches possess the most potent influences.

Once you feel a powerful sense of conviction that you have selected the most appropriate tree and branch, you are ready to prepare for the harvesting itself.

Gather together the following items:

- **A sharp knife or pruning shears.** This is used to harvest the branch from the tree in one clean cut. If you are harvesting a stave, you may need a sharp saw.

- **Your dagger.** You will use this to seal the protective Circle that you cast around the base of the donor tree.

- **A natural sealant.** You will use this to seal the branch stub left on the tree's trunk and the cut end of your harvested branch. Beeswax and pine resin are traditional sealants, but any environmentally sound commercial sealant may also be used.

- **A length of natural binding cord.** This is used to bind the newly harvested branch.

HARVESTING,
CLEANSING, AND
ENERGIZING
YOUR WAND(S)
AND STAVE

171

- **A small cloth of your choice.** You will lay your tools on the cloth during the working and then use it to wrap the newly harvested branch(es) in to transport them home.

- **A torch or lantern.** If you are harvesting by night, you'll need these.

Armed with these few essential tools, which you should cleanse and purify, along with yourself, before you leave home, you may set forth on your harvesting.

When you arrive at the donor tree, spread the cloth at the base of the tree and lay out your tools upon it.

You may choose to remove your clothing at this point. Bearing in mind that a reasonable percentage of this short ritual is concerned with combining and communicating with the collective energy and the latent energy of the donor tree, you may, like myself, think that it is appropriate to expose your natural self to the elements as you craft your working.

Standing in front of the donor tree with your stave in both hands, assume the power position of the inverted triangular pyramid. Use whatever time is necessary to raise your sensory awareness as explained earlier. When you feel prepared, move on to the next step.

Lift your stave over your head and say:

"And so it begins."

Then cast a protective Circle, as described earlier, around the donor tree. Seal the Circle with your dagger.

Sit at the base of the donor tree with your back against its trunk, making sure that the whole of your spine, including the base of the spine, is in contact with the trunk of the tree. (You may wish to sit on the cloth that you have your tools laid on.) You are about to communicate and combine with the donor tree's latent energy and, through it, the collective energy, and your spine will serve as the primary conduit for your internal energy.

As you sit, focus on the sensory experiences you heightened a moment earlier. Smell the fragrance of nature surrounding you. Feel the touch of the rough

Before harvesting your wand from the donor tree it is imperative that you connect to the latent energy of the tree itself. By sitting at the base of the tree with the base of your spine in contact with its trunk you are connecting your internal energy with that of the donor tree.

tree bark on your back. Listen to the sounds of the forest. Taste the airborne moisture and flavors carried on the wind. Close your eyes and look inward to see yourself as a part of the whole. Try and maintain all of these sensory experiences at the same time, finding a harmonic balance among them. This is the point when you "plug in" to the donor tree's energy and the collective energy. You are now all one.

Use this very special time to meditate. Visualize your harvesting, and open your senses to any negative or critical energy that may be generated by the donor tree. If you feel these are significant, abandon your harvesting and find a more suitable donor. If by the time you have completed your visualized harvesting no negative energy has been detected, retrieve your state of worldly consciousness and progress to the next step.

The next thing you are going to do is cut the branch from the donor tree. Before you begin this, set the sealant close at hand, as it is important to seal the branch stump on the tree and the cut end of your harvested branch immediately after the cut is made.

Using your knife or pruning shears, cut the branch from the donor tree about one inch from the trunk. Quickly seal the cut end of the branch stub and the cut end of the branch itself, saying:

"Thank you for your gift, I will use it well."

Trim off any extraneous twigs and leaves from the branch, immediately sealing each lesion as you progress. Place these twigs and leaves at the foot of the donor tree, saying:

"I take what you have given, and return to you what is yours. May this always be the way."

Next, loop the harvested branch so that its tip touches the cut end of its base. Bind the tip to the base using the binding cord you brought with you. Looping the branch in this manner helps it maintain its energy. Even though the ancient Druids knew nothing of electromagnetism, they still understood the concept that if something containing a force is left with its ends open, its energy quickly dissipates. (Think of the keeper strip across the poles of a horseshoe magnet.) If the

The newly harvested branch is looped over upon itself so that its tip touches the cut end of its base and is then bound in place. This retains the natural latent energy within the branch by closing its "energy loop" in order that its latent energy may continue circulating.

ends of the branch are brought together, its energy will freely circulate within it. If its ends are left open, its energy will quickly diminish.

As you will imagine, there is a risk that in looping the branch it may break or crack. If this happens, it is interpreted as a significant indicator that the branch has not been gifted to you in the proper way. Such cracked or split branches are returned to the base of the donor tree and the same words are repeated as when the surplus trimmings were placed there. (If the branch is broken or damaged while it is being crafted into a wand, then it is also returned to the donor tree in the same way.)

Hang the looped branch from the stub on the donor tree from where it was cut. Facing the donor tree and the north (therefore standing on the side opposite from where the branch was harvested), embrace the donor tree, pressing the entire front of your body against its trunk. Close your eyes and focus on receiving any negative or critical energy that the donor tree may be generating. If any is felt, return the branch to the foot of the donor tree, repeating the words given above. If you are convinced that no critical energy is being generated, walk to the other side of the donor tree and remove the looped branch from the stub where it hangs. Holding the looped branch in both hands above your head, say:

"And so it ends, at the beginning."

This ends the ritual and marks the beginning of the branch's existence as a wand. From this point on the branch takes the name of *wand*. Wrap the looped wand in cloth, gather your tools, and unseal and erase the Circle.

Cleansing: The Working

A freshly harvested wand needs to be cleaned, and this can be undertaken in a number of ways. It is not such a profound working as the regular cleansing of your cache (described in part 2), as your wand is fresh from nature, and if you harvested it in accordance with the ritual above, it will have been given freely and will harbor very few disruptive influences. The initial cleansing is more a symbolic "refreshing" of the wand, similar to the way flowers may be refreshed by changing their water and spraying them with mist.

My preferred method is to cleanse the new wand in a natural spring or stream located as close to the donor tree as possible. This feels the most natural and has worked very well for me. Having said that, I am very fortunate to live in a water-rich area that readily facilitates this method. For urban Druids this will not be a realistic option.

The most popular alternative is to cleanse the new wand at home or in your workshop using moon-cleansed water infused with purifying herbs (see part 2 for a list of purifying herbs). This is equally as effective, and having used this method many times, I can guarantee that it works perfectly well.

A newly harvested wand branch being cleansed in a mountain stream in Kerry. This stream is also the source of the spring water shown later in the moon cleansing. The end of the branch has been secured with twine and it is then left to cleanse in the running stream for two hours before being removed and dried in preparation of the next stage of its crafting. This particular rude wand was cleansed two days before the winter solstice of 2000 C.E. The wand was then used for a ritual on the evening of the solstice at the Seven Sisters circle shown previously.

In this case the actual cleansing is carried out in the same way as the cache cleansing detailed in part 2.

Crafting a Wand

Having completed the harvesting and cleansing of your new wand, the next step is its crafting.

The crafting of wands may be very simple or, as is more often the case, extremely complex. The crafting of complex wands is far beyond the purview of this book and can take many years to master. But if it is your intention to begin by crafting simple rude wands, which have a fresh, exciting energy perfectly suited to sex magic rituals, then this is a reasonably simple matter.

Rude wands are generally used more or less in the form in which they were harvested. They normally have a relatively short working life and are returned to the base of the donor tree from which they were harvested after a few hours' or days' usage.

If you intend to use rude wands for your sex magic rituals, you will have to plan a regular routine of harvesting and have a wider collection of donor trees. You cannot repeatedly harvest from the same donor tree without unsettling or damaging it in some way.

To craft a simple rude wand, all you need to do is unloop it. Make sure it is dry and clean and store it in the south/north orientation to maintain its energy until it is used. When its useful life is over and its energy depleted, return it to its donor.

Energizing: The Working

Even the most simple wand can have its potential increased by energizing. Again, this working becomes more complex as the wand itself does, but there is no reason why you should not energize the rude wand you have crafted.

If you intend to energize your wand, gently strip the bark from the surface of the wand after you unloop it. This is best done by running a sharp knife along the length of the wand shaft to create a split in the bark, then peeling back the bark gently. It's important not to cut into the wood of the wand while you're peeling it.

There is little point in sealing in all the wand's energy as you harvest it if you are then going to release it during the crafting. Carefully place the bark to one side, as you will need it later.

The energizing should be undertaken as near to the beginning of the ritual for which the wand is going to be used as possible. It is, in fact, best facilitated on the same working stone that will be used for the ritual, just hours before the ritual itself begins.

To energize your new rude wand you will need:

- **Your stave and dagger.** To cast your protective Circle and seal it.

- **An incense burner or glowing piece of charcoal in a small brazier.** Used to burn the wand's bark and generate smoke during the energizing.

- **The bark of the new wand you are going to energize.** You will burn this to produce the energizing smoke.

- **Your cauldron or a chalice.** Used to hold the moon-cleansed water.

- **Moon-cleansed water.** Used to anoint the wand.

- **Sage and lavender.** To infuse the moon-cleansed water. Sage is used for wisdom, and lavender is a particularly good herb for energizing sex magic rituals.

- **A clean white cloth.** To wipe the wand after the energizing.

Preparation for the ritual is minimal. Tie a small bunch of fresh sage and lavender together. Bruise the herbs to encourage the release of their oils and place them in the caldron of moon-cleansed water to infuse. If you do not have access to fresh herbs, tie a small amount of dried sage and lavender into a bouquet garni using a small square of muslin and suspend this in the cauldron of moon-cleansed water. Alternatively, place a few drops each of sage and lavender essential oils into the water.

Having prepared your energizing water, place it and the other items needed on your working stone.

Cast a protective Circle around the area of the working, and seal it with your dagger.

Place the burner or charcoal brazier in the center of your working stone.

HARVESTING,
CLEANSING, AND
ENERGIZING
YOUR WAND(S)
AND STAVE

179

Pick up some of the bark of the wand and place it on your heat source so that it burns slowly and produces a small plume of smoke. As you cast the first pieces of bark onto the heat source, say:

"And so it begins."

Once the plume of smoke has stabilized into a continuous flow, pick up your new wand at its base and pass its shaft back and forth through the smoke, saying:

"Borne from flame and carried through air, I call upon the energy of your own being to fill this wand with power and truth."

Remove the wand from the smoke. Refuel the smoke with more bark and repeat the process. Do this three times in total, repeating the phrase each time.

Bring the cauldron of energizing water to the front of the working stone; dip the tip of the wand into the water inside the cauldron. Take the wand out of the water and lift it vertically above your head so that the water remaining on the tip of the wand runs down its shaft. As you do this say:

"Grown from earth and cleansed by water, I call upon this draft to fill this wand with energy and wisdom."

Repeat this anointing process three times.

Pick up the dry cloth and wipe the wand, moving from base to tip, three times. As you wipe it for the third and final time say:

"And so it ends."

Place the wand aside on the working stone, setting it in the south/north orientation. It is now fully empowered and ready for your impending ritual.

Unseal and erase your Circle, remove the tools of the wand-energizing working, and prepare your working stone for the ritual to follow.

Creating Your Binding Vessel: The Working

The binding vessel is an essential element of any working or ritual involving more than one participant.

If you are solely a hedge Druid, you will not need a binding vessel. A hedge Druid, like a hedge witch, is a Druid who practices only in the seclusion of his or her own home or workshop. The expression "hedge Druid" most likely derives from the early Christian times when practicing Druids (and witches) were persecuted, and they grew tall hedges around their homes and workshops to hide their activities from the view of outsiders.

The purpose of the binding vessel is to bind together the participants of a Gathering, working, or ritual. In binding the participants, the vessel acts both as a permanent symbol of the individual participants' commitment to the group and as a means of binding all the participants' internal energies together in a potent symbiotic state. It amplifies the power of each individual by drawing on the combined power of the group.

The binding vessel is a container that holds the amalgamated compound of donations of earth given by each participant in the Gathering. The container may be very simple and crude or extremely elaborate and flamboyant. As it is going to be containing elemental energies, it must be made from a material that has calming, protective attributes. Silver and blue glass are good choices, as they are associated with the calming, cool influences of the lunar/female aspect.

The vessel is going to be sealed with wax, so select a container that is appropriate for this kind of treatment. It is going to contain a finely ground dust, so either it should have a reasonably wide neck, allowing the dust to be poured directly into the vessel, or you should have a funnel of some sort to help fill the vessel.

The binding vessel becomes influential only when all the participants who have contributed their individual earth donations are present. The binding vessel belongs to the particular Gathering that contributed to it. It has no value to any other group. If one of the contributors is missing from the Gathering, then the binding vessel is useless. If any additional participants are present who have not donated to the vessel's contents, it then becomes passive.

You will realize, then, that the binding vessel, although a potent working tool, is suitable only for Gatherings that meet regularly and always contain the same participants. It is a tool that can only be used effectively by a Gathering with a long-standing, well-established membership.

The process of creating a binding vessel is not a complicated one, but it must be done over at least two consecutive Gatherings. Once the Gathering has agreed that it is appropriate for them to create a binding vessel, the priest or priestess issues the invitation to all participants to contribute donations of earth compounds. He or she explains that each participant is required to collect a small amount of earth from a place that has great significance to him or her. It may be from their home garden, a special place in a local woodland, a secluded meditation spot— anywhere that the participant relates to in a powerful way. The earth should be collected at a meaningful time; this is up to the individual, but it is usual for males to collect in the sunlight and females to collect in moonlight. Each individual earth donation should be no more than a thimbleful of fine, soft earth; you will not want a binding vessel the size of an oil drum once you have put all the donations together. The donation can be contained in whatever feels appropriate to the individual, whether a small pouch, a small metal or wood container, a glass vial, or so on.

The Gathering agrees to reassemble at a later date, at which time all its participants bring their donation. The next stage is the giving and taking of the donations. This is a very brief affair and normally takes place at the beginning or the end of a Gathering convened for a larger purpose. The priest or priestess stands facing the Gathering with his or her back to the working stone, usually holding a receptacle of some sort. In turn, the participants walk past the priest or priestess. As they arrive, he or she asks:

A group of participants at a Gathering offering their donations of earth compounds to the priestess in order for her to craft their binding vessel.

"Is this donation given freely and in the knowledge of the purpose of its use?"

The participant replies:

"Yes, it is given freely and I understand the purpose of its use."

The participant then drops the earth donation into the receptacle and moves on to allow the next participant to approach. This continues until all the donations are received. The priest or priestess then places the receptacle aside.

Later, in the seclusion of his or her workshop, the priest or priestess undertakes the binding working.

For this working you will need:

- **Your chosen binding vessel (empty at this stage).** This will contain your binding compound.

- **A pestle and mortar.** Used to grind the earth compound into a fine, dry dust.

- **Your cauldron or a similar heatproof dish.** Used to hold the wet binding compound over your heat source before it is placed in the binding vessel.

- **Heat source.** Must be able to stand safely on the top of your working stone. Used to heat the cauldron or heatproof dish.

- **A wooden mixing spoon.** Used to combine the various earth donations in the cauldron.

- **A second vessel.** Must be large enough to hold the combined donations of earth. Used to contain the compound during the working.

- **Wax.** Used to seal your binding vessel. Use sealing wax or similar hard-drying wax.

- **Natural binding (such as raffia or hemp).** Used to tie a triple-knotted seal around the neck or top of the vessel. You will need a short length (about 12 inches).

- **Moon-cleansed water.** To form a paste of your compound.

- **Your stave and dagger.** To cast and seal your protective Circle.

- **A small white cleansing cloth.** Used to clean the binding vessel after it has been filled.

The Gathering's earth compound donations are first mixed together and then finely ground in a mortar and pestle. This grinding both reduces the size of the aggregate in the compound, thereby aiding the blending of the assembled compounds, and allows the priest or priestess to energize the compound before sealing it in the binding vessel.

To begin the working, cast and seal the Circle in the usual manner.

When this is complete, place the cauldron in the middle of the front of the working stone. Open each donation and pour it into the cauldron. Be absolutely certain that the cauldron contains the donations of each and every participant in the Gathering. Leaving out just one donation will negate the whole working.

Using the wooden spoon, mix together the donations.

There follows a series of mixing and grinding processes that can be very tedious to say the least. A repetitive chant recited through the process can help the priest or priestess maintain focus. You can, and should, compose your own for this purpose. I use, "Binding creates greater power."

Make sure your chant is not too long or complicated or all your focus will go toward remembering it and not into your working.

Transfer the compound to the mortar and grind it with the pestle until a fine, smooth dusty consistency is achieved. This can take some time, sometimes even hours. Try to maintain your focus throughout; visualize the binding together of the Gathering concerned and the powerful energy that the binding will create.

The motive behind the grinding is to mix the individual donations to the finest degree possible. This makes the earth particles smaller so they achieve greater contact with one another.

Once the desired fineness is achieved, return the compound to the cauldron and add enough moon-cleansed water to turn the dry powder into a thick paste.

Mix the paste thoroughly with the wooden spoon, then remove the spoon, making sure every drop of the paste is returned to the cauldron. Using the pestle, grind the paste to an even finer consistency. When the desired fineness is achieved, remove the pestle, again returning every speck of the paste to the cauldron.

You should now have a thick fine paste at the bottom of your cauldron. The next step is to dry it out.

Place the cauldron over your heat source. The liquid will eventually evaporate from the paste, leaving a hard film on the inside and base of your cauldron. Remove the cauldron from the heat, allow it to cool, and place it back on your work surface.

Use the pestle to regrind the dry paste back into a fine powder. The finer, the better. (You can begin to see now why this working is not repeated too often. It takes a good deal of time and effort.) It is crucial that you incorporate all of the residual paste back into the finished compound.

Once you are happy that the compound is sufficiently mixed and ground, place your second vessel on your work surface. Lifting the cauldron about 8 inches above the second vessel, slowly pour the dry powder from the cauldron into the second vessel. Once the entire compound is transferred, place the cauldron on the work surface, pick up the second vessel, and pour the compound from the second vessel back into the cauldron. This separates the grains of the powder and incorporates air into the compound. Repeat this process three times in total.

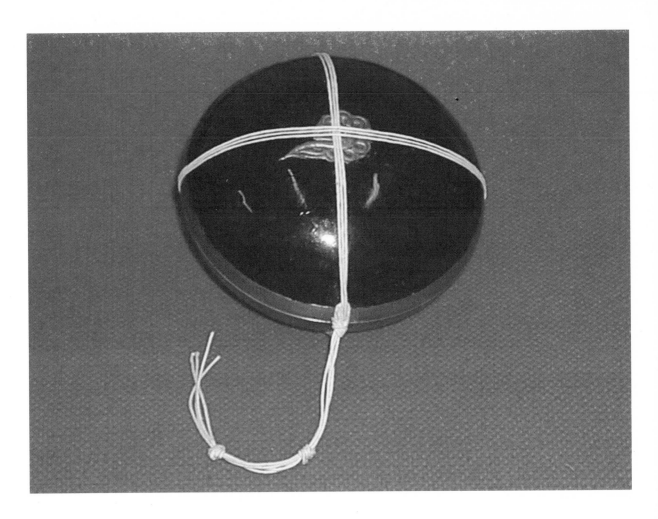

A sealed binding vessel containing the earth compounds donated by the participants of a specific Gathering. This binding vessel has a role to play only if all the participants who donated compounds to its crafting are present at the rituals where it is used. A priest or priestess may be in possession of a number of different binding vessels, each created for one of the many Gatherings over which he or she may preside.

You will have noticed that all four of the basic elements have been incorporated into this binding working. The compound itself comes from the earth; water was used to further bind the compound; fire was used to evaporate the water and purify the compound; and air was used to separate and further cleanse the compound.

Transfer the finished compound to the binding vessel and secure the vessel's top with a cap, cork, or lid. Make sure that every last grain of the compound is in the binding vessel before you secure the top.

Seal the cork, cap, or lid with the sealing wax. Some people choose to cover the whole cap. Others place three "blobs" of sealing wax equally spaced around the cap. If you choose the second method, make sure the blobs of wax straddle the joint of the vessel and the cap in such a way as to prevent the vessel from being opened without breaking the seal.

Finally, wind the natural cord three times around the neck of the vessel and tie it in three knots visible from the front of the vessel. Allow the trailing ends of the cord to dangle at the front of the vessel.

As the third knot in the sealing cord is tied, say:

"And so it begins."

Give the vessel a final cleaning with the cloth. Now your binding vessel is complete and ready to be presented to the Gathering when it is next convened. In the meantime, store the binding vessel with the other items in your cache. Erase the Circle in the usual manner.

This is a traditional method of symbolically sealing a vessel or container. No Druid would ever open a container sealed by another with a triple-knotted cord. Only the same Druid can end what he or she begins.

You can have more than one binding vessel; in fact, at the moment I have seven. Each one belongs to a different Gathering. If you do have more than one binding vessel, mark each one in some way to identify which Gathering it belongs to. I place a small sticky label on the base of each vessel.

As soon as a binding vessel ceases to represent the current group of individuals in the Gathering that it binds together, it becomes useless. In this eventuality the priest or priestess who created it removes the seal, opens the vessel, and pours its contents on the ground. This is a relatively unimportant working, but it should be conducted with the appropriate reverence in a quiet, secluded spot. As the contents are poured onto the ground, the priest or priestess says:

"I return to the earth what is the earth. And so it ends."

The vessel and the sealing cord may then be cleansed and purified in the usual way and used again for another Gathering.

Moon-Cleansed Water: The Working

Moon-cleansed water forms the core of many workings and is involved in one way or another with nearly every activity the Druidic priest or priestess undertakes. It is not difficult to make, although its creation may disrupt your sleeping pattern a little.

For this working you will need:

- **A supply of fresh springwater.** Draw it yourself from a freshwater spring or purchase natural springwater (still, not sparkling) at a store.

- **A clear glass bottle or container.** Used to hold the springwater during the moon cleansing. Should be cleansed, purified, and sterilized before the working.

- **Blue glass bottles or containers.** Have enough to hold the amount of springwater you are cleansing. Should be cleansed, purified, and sterilized before the working.

Begin with good-quality bottled springwater. If you have a source of fresh springwater close to you, consider using it, particularly if it is drawn from a place that you have an affinity for. Remember, though, that you and the other participants in your rituals will sometimes consume this water. So unless you are absolutely sure that your source is pure, unpolluted, and safe to drink, stick to the bottled springwater.

You will need to plan your cleansing working to coincide with a "fat" moon. A fat moon is apparent a few days before, during, and after the full moon, when the visible moon is at its largest and emits the maximum amount of moonlight. This is generally a very good time to facilitate your sex magic rituals, particularly

Moon-cleansed water forms the basis of many Druidic rituals and may also be the main ingredient of many Druidic potions and remedies. Here we see a flask of spring water at moonrise. The flask sits on a standing stone in the garden of my home in Kerry where it will remain until just before dawn the following morning, at which time it is decanted into a blue glass vessel for storage before the sun rises.

those held outdoors and those involving predominantly female participants. Every Druidic priestess is most active in her workings and rituals during the fat moon phase. It is also an excellent time for group sex magic rituals with a female Principal Conduit. If a priestess also facilitates the ritual, the generated energy can be extremely potent indeed.

The moon-cleansing working begins at dusk, or, more accurately, as soon as the moonlight is visible. The cleansing process is very simple. If you have drawn your water from a local source, just seal it in a sterilized, clear glass bottle and place it outside in a location where it is exposed to the maximum amount of moonlight. I place mine on top of two standing stones that I have in my garden. In the morning, before the sun rises, decant the cleansed water into a sterilized blue glass bottle and seal it.

If you are using store-bought springwater, simply remove the label from the bottle by soaking it in water for a few minutes and then peeling. This gives the moonlight access to more of the water in the bottle. Then place the bottle outside as explained above. There is no need to break the seal on the bottle until you decant it just before dawn.

Store the moon-cleansed water in its blue glass bottle or container until you are ready to use it. It becomes part of your cache and will be cleansed and purified regularly along with your other tools.

Salt: The Working

Salt has long been used as a preservative and purifying agent and used to be, and in some regions still is, of considerable value. People were often even paid for their work in salt, hence the word "salary" and the expression "He's worth his salt."

The magical properties of salt have been acknowledged since the dawn of the Druidic tradition, and it has been used as a cleansing and purifying agent ever since. It also plays a large role in the healing practices of the Druidic tradition.

In the Welsh tradition, salt is evaporated from seawater not mined from the earth. Sea salt contains, in addition to the basic salt, minerals that fix additional influences and benefits in the compound.

If you can obtain fresh seawater that is clean and unpolluted, you can make your own sea salt, and this should always be your first choice. I collect seawater from the western coast of Ireland, where I live, and it makes wonderful salt. When I lived in Wales, I found it difficult to find a reliable source of unpolluted seawater without traveling for miles to collect it. If you cannot obtain clean seawater, the major brands of commercial sea salt are guaranteed to be unpolluted and work effectively.

The working for harvesting salt from fresh seawater is as follows.

For this working you will need:

- **A supply of clean seawater.** For evaporating salt from.
- **Your cauldron or similar heatproof bowl.** To hold the seawater over the heat source.
- **A heat source capable of evaporating the seawater.** I use a campstove.
- **A metal spoon (preferably silver).** For scraping the salt from your cauldron.
- **An airtight receptacle.** For storing your harvested salt.

Here we see the tools necessary for a small-scale salt evaporation working. The collected seawater is stored in the blue glass vessel. It will be poured into the small crucible and evaporated over the heat source leaving the salt residue in the base of the vessel. The copper spoon is used to draw the salt deposits from the sides and base of the crucible, and the small wooden pestle and mortar is used to grind the salt crystals into a fine powder before it is stored.

This is a time-consuming process, so do not attempt to evaporate too much seawater at each session.

To begin, place your cauldron over your heat source and allow it to heat up. Pour or ladle about half a cupful of seawater into the cauldron. It will sizzle and splatter as you pour it in, so be very careful. It should evaporate quickly and leave a fine whitish deposit on the bottom of your cauldron. Before this burns and turns brown, add another half-cup of seawater and allow it to evaporate in the same manner, leaving a slightly thicker layer on the bottom of your cauldron. Continue in the same manner, adding more seawater, letting it evaporate, and accumulating a thicker and thicker deposit of salt on the bottom of your cauldron.

When you judge the salt deposit to be of a sufficient thickness to gather, scrape the deposit off the cauldron using the metal spoon. If you prefer, grind the salt to a more even consistency with a mortar and pestle. Store the salt in an airtight container. Continue this process until you have collected all the salt you need. Your salt canister becomes part of your cache.

The purifying attributes of the salt are such that no Circle is usually required for this working, unless the person doing the working feels threatened. This working may also be done in the "background" while you are undertaking other workings; take care not to let the salt burn, though, as it turns an unattractive shade of brownish-black and cannot then be used.

SALT: THE
WORKING

Initiation and Naming: The Rituals

Initiation is a crucial part of every individual's path through the tradition. This section deals with initiation and naming in relation to sex magic rituals only. This should not be confused with initiation into the full Druidic tradition; that is a much more complex and binding ritual.

Initiation and naming are normally facilitated at the same ritual, usually as part of a Gathering for a larger purpose. The most significant part of the initiation ritual is the naming of the initiate. This is the point in the ritual when the initiate is given his or her Druidic name. This Druidic name stays with the initiate for the remainder of his or her life.

There is a school of thought that in recent years has suggested a newly hatched idea of "self-initiation." If during the course of this section you gain an understanding of the principles of initiation and naming, then I suggest that you will have to agree that the concept of self-initiation is both unsustainable and ill conceived.

As there is no "International University of Druidism" that is able to validate official qualifications in Druidic studies, individuals are free to proclaim themselves Druids, Druidic priests, or any other title that takes their fancy. Hence the slightly amusing declarations of Druidic Ph.D.s (Practicing Holistic Druid, would you believe) and the more worrying self-professed Arch Druids and Druids appearing in the strangest parts of the world. Self-profession, along with self-initiation, has been introduced by individuals who have no real contact with the tradition. To gain a sense of belonging, they have invented these fanciful declarations in order to project some vain sense of acquired learning and self-esteem.

The point is that Druidism is about acquiring knowledge, skills, and attitudes that enable you to practice the tradition; it is not about self-manufactured qualifications. In fact, as Druidism has an oral tradition of teaching and learning, there have never been any Druidic qualifications and, most likely, never will be.

The idea of self-initiation is particularly contradictory to the tradition. Initiation is the acceptance of the initiate into a teaching/learning relationship with the mature Druid. The mature Druid in turn accepts the initiate into his or her care and undertakes to begin and continue the training of the initiate in the tradition. As very little if any of the true Druidic tradition is recorded, the only way to learn the various aspects of the tradition is still from a mature Druid via the oral tradition.

If you become a self-initiate, you are placing yourself into your own care and giving yourself the responsibility for teaching yourself the Druidic tradition. As very little of the true tradition is actually recorded, it must then be the case that, if you are going to teach it to yourself, you already know the bulk of it. In this case, why are you an initiate?

Self-initiation simply does not stand up to scrutiny.

The only way to become an initiate is to bind yourself to a mature Druid or Druidess. His or her only qualification and claim to the title of Druid is the history of his or her training/learning relationship with a Druidic tutor, his or her knowledge of the oral tradition, and his or her acceptance by the community as a practicing Druid.

How then, do you become an initiate into the practices of Celtic sex magic? Sex magic is a very powerful tool, but it is only a very, very small part of the Druidic tradition. Like many of the other Druidic practices it may be exercised as an individual craft. Traditionally, Druids appointed specific priests and priestesses to facilitate limited rituals on their behalf. Having received adequate instruction, these priests and priestesses often worked as independent practitioners in their own disciplines. In creating this book, I have compiled and detailed the essential "knowledge and instruction" required to enable you to practice sex magic in a safe and disciplined way. With sufficient effort and understanding you may become a practicing priest or priestess involving yourself only in the practice of sex magic. This is not an act of self-profession; it is a description of what you will be doing.

INITIATION
AND NAMING:
THE RITUALS

In accepting initiates into your Gathering, you are accepting individuals into your group of practicing sex magic participants; you are not initiating them into the Druidic tradition. That, as you will now understand, is a very different matter. The sex magic initiation is, then, simply an acceptable and useful way of accepting new individuals into your Gathering.

Naming is an important concept in initiation. Druidic tradition holds that knowing the name of someone or something gives you some form of power over it. To put this profound principle into everyday terms, by knowing someone's name you exercise some form of power over him or her.

This is easily tested. If you see someone you know in a large crowd, you would not just shout, "Hey there!" to attract his or her attention; instead, you would call his or her name. This causes them to turn toward you. You have exercised power in making them aware of your presence by using their name.

What if you are given inadequate change by someone you know who works in a local store? Telling someone that you were "short-changed by some guy in that store" has a very different effect from saying, "Tom short-changed me." Tom becomes a wrong-doer.

These are simple examples, and given a few moments I am sure you will be able to think of many more. But they serve the purpose of demonstrating the power contained in knowing a name. This simple power serves as the basis for two Druidic principles that predetermine teaching and learning relationships in the tradition. The first is the concept that, before you invoke any power, you must fully understand it and the consequences of its use. The second is that you must know the meaning and uses of a thing before you are given its name.

The first of these is relatively easy to understand in relation to naming. Before you use the name of anything or anyone, you must understand the reason for his, her, or its existence and the consequence of invoking his, her, or its name.

The second is much more profound and forms the basis of the whole teaching/learning relationship within the tradition. It is most easily explained by a basic comparison.

Let us imagine that we have been given the task of explaining what a wand is to someone who has never seen or heard of one before. We might say:

"A wand is a piece of wood about 12 inches long. It has been harvested from a tree and contains the specific characteristic attributes of the tree from which it was cut. It is used to focus energy and influence that energy with its natural intrinsic attributes."

This is a reasonable description of a wand, offering a physical description of the wand, its origin, and its use. But consider how a Druid might offer a description to a student:

"If you want to focus and channel energy and influence it in a specific way, you first find a tree that has the natural attributes that correspond to the way you wish to influence the energy you intend to channel. Then you cut from the tree a slim branch about 12 inches long. This branch is then cleansed, purified, and energized in order to make it an effective and versatile tool for Druidic rituals and workings."

"Do you understand this?"

Only when the individual says yes does the teacher proceed with, "Then I shall tell you that this tool is called a wand."

Only once the individual knows and acknowledges that he or she understands the meaning and uses of a wand is he or she given its name.

You will see as we progress that these principles are essential to the initiation and naming ritual that follows.

Initiation and naming are based on three principles:

1. The initiation is the acceptance of the initiate into the sex magic Gathering as a full participant in all future activities.

2. The initiate must be known to all the participants of the Gathering, and his or her motives for becoming a participant must be understood by everyone before he or she may be named.

3. After being named, the initiate becomes a permanent participant in the Gathering and all the other participants will know the initiate's name.

The name given to the initiate will be decided by the priest or priestess prior to the ritual. It will be a name used only in the context of future sex magic rituals. During the ritual the name is told secretly to the initiate; the initiate tells the

Gathering of his or her own free will. In giving his or her name to the Gathering, the initiate gives each individual of the Gathering the power associated with knowing his or her name.

Traditionally, the name relates to a natural feature that the priest or priestess feels is reflected in the personality of the initiate. It may be the name of a river (as in my case), a flower, or any natural phenomenon that the priest or priestess feels is appropriate. Once given, it is never changed.

The initiation and naming ritual is conducted as follows.

Preparation

The priest or priestess interviews the initiate in private on a number of occasions. The interview is used to get to know the initiate as well as possible before he or she is accepted into the gathering. The priest or priestess ascertains:

- The sincerity of the intiate's motives for wishing to become involved in sex magic gatherings

- That he or she has a good basic understanding of the fundamental principles involved

- That he or she is of good character, law abiding, and trustworthy

- That he or she is mentally and physically up to the tasks ahead

- That he or she is healthy and free from infection

Some argue that there should be exploratory sexual contact between the initiate and the priest or priestess in order to ascertain the initiate's sexual experience, ability, and preferences. I feel that this can be achieved through conversation, and I prefer to avoid actual sexual contact with initiates as it has a certain illicit "cult-ish" feel to it and leaves the priest or priestess open to all sorts of accusations and threats, particularly if the initiate is then not accepted into the Gathering.

These interviews also provide the opportunity for the priest or priestess to explain to the initiate what will be required of him or her during the initiation and naming and the sequence of events as they unfold during the ritual itself.

If the candidate is acceptable to the priest or priestess, he or she announces at the end of a Gathering that an initiate will be presented at the next meeting.

The priest or priestess then plans the next Gathering to incorporate the initiation and naming ritual at the beginning of the activities.

The priest or priestess meets with the initiate to go over in detail the actual events of the ritual, and the initiate is told where and when the ritual is to take place and to wear a loose-fitting robe (a somber dressing gown is suitable) to the Gathering.

The Ritual

Once the Circle has been cast and sealed and the usual preparations for a ritual have been completed, the priest or priestess stands before the working stone and announces:

"There is one among us who wishes to join our Gathering. Let him [or her] step forward and make himself [or herself] known."

The initiate steps forward to stand in front of the priest or priestess and says:

"I am he [or she]. I wish to join this Gathering."

The priest or priestess says:

"I know you and acknowledge your intention. Will you answer to the Gathering?"

The initiate says:

"I will."

The initiate then turns to face the assembled Gathering in the Circle. The priest or priestess asks the following questions of the initiate, and he or she answers as follows:

P: "Are your intentions pure and truthful?"

I: "They are."

P: "Do you understand your commitment?"

I: "I do, and I commit myself to you."

P: "Will you hold our efforts in high esteem and keep them secret to yourself?"

I: *"I will honor your trust in me."*

The priest or priestess, still facing the Gathering, then says:

"You have before you the initiate. He [or she] presents himself [herself] for your acceptance. Will you know him [her]?"

As the priest or priestess says these words, the initiate removes his or her robe and stands naked before the Gathering. The disrobing is a symbol of unity with the other participants, who are already naked, and demonstrates that nothing is hidden or stands between the initiate and his or her intention to join the Gathering.

The participants respond as a body:

"We will know him [or her]."

The initiate walks to the convocation stone and lies upon it in the south/north orientation.

The participants of the Gathering now assemble around the convocation stone and lay their hands on the initiate. This may take the form of a simple symbolic touch by some; others will explore the initiate's body in more detail. It may be no more than a series of hands briefly touching the initiate's body, or it may develop into a simplistic Projection Cycle resulting in the initiate's orgasm projecting his intention to become part of the Gathering.

It is also an opportunity for the participants of the Gathering to get to know a little about the initiate's sexual preferences and sensitive areas.

Once the priest or priestess judges that sufficient time has been given to this part of the ritual, he or she says:

"I will name the initiate."

The participants draw away from the convocation stone and return to their original positions in the Circle.

The priest or priestess walks to the initiate's head, and standing behind the convocation stone and facing north, he or she takes hold of the initiate's

The priestess bends over the initiate and whispers his Druidic name into his ear. The initiate is lying on the convocation stone in the center of the Circle with his feet pointing north toward the working stone.

shoulders in both hands, leans forward, and whispers the initiate's name into his or her ear as follows:

"I give you the name of _____ . Do you accept it?"

The initiate replies:

"Yes, I accept the name of _____."

The priest or priestess then returns to the working stone, and as he or she does so, the initiate rises and follows. Standing next to the initiate and facing the Gathering, the priest or priestess says:

"He [or she] is named. Will you know how to call him [or her]?"

The Gathering replies:

"Yes, we would know how."

The initiate says:

"My name is _____, I greet you."

The Gathering and the priest or priestess say:

"Welcome _____. Join us and become one with us."

At this point the initiate walks to join the Gathering. As he or she does so, the Gathering usually claps hands or sings a song of welcome.

The Sex Magic Ritual: The Pair

Probably the sex magic ritual practiced most often, the paired ritual both is an opportunity to develop your awareness and skills and, when conducted correctly, is capable of generating enormous energy.

It is usually the case that practiced pairs are the most effective, committed, and valuable participants in a Gathering. They form the basis of most regular groups, and if you were to conduct a detailed census I am sure that the bulk of existing binding vessels contain earth compounds donated by practiced pairs.

Having practiced pairs in a Gathering is ideal for all concerned. It alleviates the task of the priest or priestess to institute gender balance, it ensures a high level of participation at Gatherings, and, as these pairs often become regular participants, it allows the priest or priestess to develop the Gathering as a group with common goals and well-understood practices.

If, in addition to their enthusiasm for being involved with each other, the paired individuals also share an enthusiasm for becoming involved with other individuals and pairs, then all the better.

You will find that as the Gathering divides into groups during the sex magic ritual, the practiced pairs will be the basis for the formation of larger active groups within the gathering. However, there must always be the opportunity for these pairs to participate between themselves, without including any additional group members.

Putting these group advantages to one side, we must look at the sex magic ritual as conducted between two individuals.

There are basically two formats for paired individuals: one priest or priestess and a participant, or one priest and one priestess. The relationship and commitment of the two individuals involved often determines this. If only one of the individuals is interested and committed enough to develop their knowledge, skills, and attitudes sufficiently to undertake the role of Druidic priest or priestess, but the other is interested enough to be an active participant, then their roles are determined for them. If both have equal commitment and dedication, they may work together as priest and priestess or exchange roles as they see fit.

However, for every ritual there must be a dominant role (that of priest or priestess) and a cooperative role (that of active participant). In the case of the paired ritual there must be a priest or priestess to facilitate the ritual and a Principal Conduit through whom the generated energy will be projected.

The priest or priestess will provide the majority of the stimulation, and his or her orgasm, although secondary to that of the Principal Conduit, should be synchronized with it. The Principal Conduit will be stimulated to the peak of his or her sensory potential, and his or her orgasm will project the generated energy carrying the spell to its recipient.

In the case of a male/female pairing, it makes no difference which partner undertakes which role. Many couples change roles regularly; others prefer to maintain the same roles on every occasion. You will find that there is a natural balance to the pairing; one partner will be more suited to a particular role than the other. As you become more familiar with the sex magic ritual you will discover this natural balance, but continue to experiment and exchange roles until you feel that balance has been achieved. Your eventual role will reflect the major aspects of your personality and the aspects of your relationship with your partner. In the case of gay or lesbian couples the natural balance will follow the same trends.

The roles you adopt will often be the same as they are in your everyday sexual relationship. If the female is the dominant partner in the usual sexual relationship, then, all other things being equal, it is likely that she will develop into the role of priestess and the male partner into the role of Principal Conduit. If the male is the dominant sexual partner, then the opposite will apply.

It is important to remember, however, that both "roles" (and that word is

again a poor translation from its Welsh equivalent) are equally important. Neither can function to their full potential without the collaboration of the other.

For the purpose of this example, we will assume that a priestess is facilitating the ritual and that the Principal Conduit is the male. You can then superimpose your circumstances upon the workings as appropriate.

For this ritual you will need:

- **Your wand(s).** Used in all your rituals.

- **Your stave.** To cast your first Circle.

- **Your salt canister.** To cast your Second Circle. Should contain sufficient salt for the purpose.

- **Your hand-held candle.** To cast your third Circle.

- **Your dagger.** To seal the Circle, along with the salt and candle above.

- **Your cauldron, filled with moon-cleansed water.** For the purification activities within the ritual.

- **Two floor-standing candleholders.** To create the portal within your Circle. The flames of these two candles will be at shoulder height.

- **Three working stone candles, in candleholders.** The center focus of your working stone.

- **Your phallus.** For stimulation during the ritual. Use a number of phalluses if you have them, together with the necessary condoms needed to ensure hygiene.

- **Your binding vessel.** Most couples create a binding vessel early on in their involvement to unite their individual energies.

- **Incense burners or essential oil evaporators.** To enhance the atmosphere of the ritual and invest the working with the attributes of the herbs used.

- **Cleansing cloths.** As many as you feel are necessary.

The ritual begins with the priestess raising her sensory awareness using the inverted triangular pyramid working. She then casts a triple-cast Circle of a suitable size. As each of the two participants enters the Circle, they extend their arms to each side, level with their shoulders, passing each hand quickly through

The lighting of candles plays a significant part in all Druidic practices. What must be remembered, however, is that it is the flame that is significant and not the candle itself. The central flame represents the collective energy; the outer flames represent the energies of the sun and moon.

the flames of the two portal candles, a symbolic final purification of the body. Once both are inside the Circle, the priestess seals the Circle with the triple seal. Both participants are now enclosed within the protective Circle and are ready to begin the sex magic ritual.

The Principal Conduit sits on the ground facing the working stone.

The priestess stands before the working stone and brings the first of the candles, the collective energy candle, to the front of the stone. She lights the candle, raises it into the air, and says:

"As this flame burns, so we converge with the collective energy. Our energies mingle, our potential becomes one."

The "flame of the collective energy" candle is placed at the back, in the center, of the working stone.

The priestess then lights the sun, or male, candle, holds it up, and says:

"As this flame burns it bind us with the sun. We invoke the sun's influence upon our workings."

The "flame of the sun" candle is placed to the left and slightly forward of the "flame of the collective energy" candle.

She then lights the third and final moon or female candle, holds it up, and says:

"As this flame burns I bind myself with the moon. I invoke the moon's influence upon all I do."

The "flame of the moon" candle is placed to the right and slightly in front of the "flame of the collective energy" candle, forming the candle triangle.

You will see that this third invocation is a personal one. If the ritual is facilitated by the male, then the moon candle is lit before the sun candle, and this same personal invocation is given for the sun candle.

With all three candle flames lit, the priestess stands before them at the front/center of the working stone and extends her arms out so that each of her palms is directly above each of the sun and moon flames, close enough to feel the heat of the flames without burning her palms. She then brings both hands together above the central collective energy flame to form a "cup" shape above the flame, saying:

"I unite all things with the collective energy, as in nature they belong. I offer myself to this union, together with all those present here. Unite us in your common bond."

This opening part of the ritual, called the "uniting of the flames," is now complete.

If the pair has a previously crafted binding vessel, the priestess now lifts it aloft, saying:

"This binding vessel binds all present to one. I now bind it to the united flames as a symbol of our affinity."

The "male" wand enters the "female" cauldron in symbolic representation of the union of the male and female elements of creation. As it enters, the water ripples appear on the surface, emanating from the tip of the wand, representing the emanation of the Principal Conduit's spell into the cosmos.
The priest or priestess invokes "only what is good and beneficial" and banishes "all that is unwelcome."

She passes the binding vessel quickly through each of the three flames, then places it in the center of the candle triangle, at the base of the "flame of the collective energy" candle. As we have seen previously, the center point of a triangle is a power point.

The preparation of the working stone is now complete. The priestess must now prepare the convocation stone to receive the Principal Conduit.

Picking up her wand in her right hand (or in her left if she is left-handed), the priestess moves to the convocation stone. Extending her wand above the stone, she walks around it three times, saying quietly to herself:

"I invoke only what is good, I intend only what is beneficial, I banish all that is unwelcome."

The priestess then returns to the working stone, picks up the cauldron with the moon-cleansed water, and returns to the convocation stone. Again she walks three times around the stone, but this time she dips the tip of the wand into the water and sprinkles drops of it on the stone as she walks. She again says:

"I invoke only what is good, I intend only what is beneficial, I banish all that is unwelcome."

She returns the cauldron to the working stone and stands with her back to it, facing the center of the Circle. She says, in a loud voice:

"Come forward who wishes to lie here."

The Principal Conduit approaches the priestess and says:

"That is I."

The priestess says:

"And are you named?"

If the Principal Conduit has already been named, then his name is spoken. We shall use the name "David" for the sake of this example.

The Principal Conduit (David) says:

"Yes, my name is David. I wish to lie here."

The priestess says:

"Then as I know your name to be David, take your place as it is offered."

David then takes his place on the convocation stone, with his head at the center point of the Circle and his feet facing the working stone. This means that he is lying in the south/north orientation, so the energies will flow through him from his head to his feet, aiding the projection of generated energy from his body.

The priestess now stands between the two stones, facing the center of the Circle, and says:

"I welcome all those that wish us well. We are gathered with the intention of creating change. Change that offers benefit and goodwill. Our spell is crafted and I offer it to you."

She then speaks the spell for the first time. The Gathering, in this case just her partner, already knows the spell and will have committed it to memory. For the sake of simplicity we shall just call it "the spell."

The priestess says:

"The spell."

The Principal Conduit repeats the spell three times:

"The spell; the spell; the spell."

The priestess, picking up her wand and cauldron, walks to the convocation stone where the Principal Conduit now lies and says:

"Our Principal Conduit is David. Through him we shall cast and bind our spell."

She sprinkles the Principal Conduit with the moon-cleansed water, using her wand to do so. As she does this, she says:

"I anoint you, David, and commit my efforts to your internal energy."

The cauldron and the wand are placed back on the working stone and the Projection Cycle begins.

As the seven successions of the Projection Cycle have been explained in detail in part 2, we will concentrate here on the more physical aspects of the ritual.

As the pair progress through the first three successions—the Awakening, Augmentation, and Intensification—a variety of techniques may be employed to arouse and stimulate both the Principal Conduit and the priestess.

What follows is just an example of a typical progression to use as a guide. There is no set format to this part of the ritual; it is up to the priestess to judge the most appropriate and effective methods. Each priestess will develop her own repertoire of techniques and actions together with a sensibility in relation to what is or is not acceptable.

The Awakening usually involves a gentle and sensuous awakening of the sexual senses. It may involve the use of massage, oils, lotions, creams, and the like, applied to the bodies and genitals of both the Principal Conduit and the priestess. These may be applied by hand and exchanged bodily massage. It can also involve gentle oral stimulation of the sensitive areas and genitalia.

This is always a slow build-up of sexual awareness and a gentle introduction to the pleasures to come, and it should result only in a simple arousal. It is the opportunity to get to know your own body and that of your partner in the ritual.

PERFORMING
WORKINGS
AND RITUALS

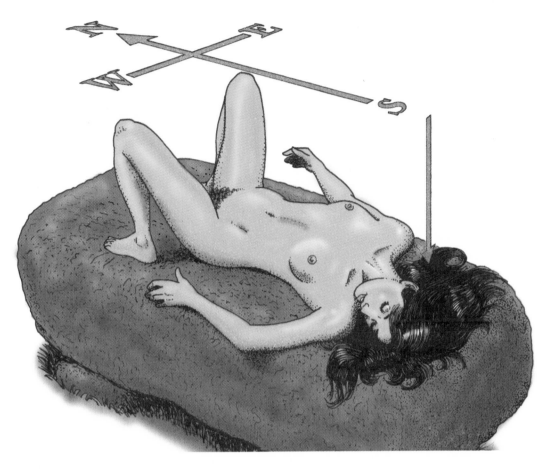

The orientation of the Principal Conduit, shown in this case as a female, is crucial both to the harnessing and utilization of the earth's energies and to the integrity of the working area of the protective Circle. Both of these factors are defined by the cardinal points of the compass. The arrow pointing at the Principal Conduit's head indicates the center point of the protective Circle, where the Conduit's head should be located in order to focus the Circle's energy.

The emphasis is on slow, sensual movement and gentle physical contact with fingertips, tongue, nipples, lips, and so on. It can be enhanced by the use of perfumed oils, incense, and sensual music.

As the ritual progresses to the Augmentation succession, the form of stimulation may change. The slow sensuality may become more physical. At this stage both the Principal Conduit and the priestess will be masturbating themselves and each other. Individuals may now part company in order to provide their partner with more visual stimuli. This can range form watching each other masturbate and stimulate themselves to using the phallus on and in themselves to erotic dance and other forms of exhibitionism.

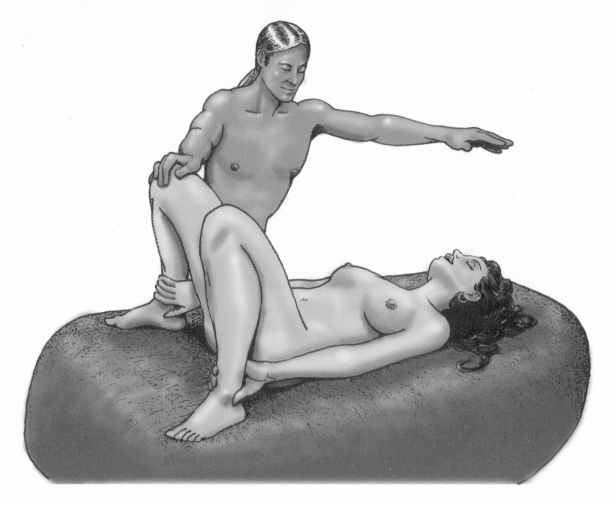

All Celtic sex magic rituals are facilitated equally as effectively by the pair as they are within a larger Gathering. In many cases paired couples may choose to conduct these rituals in the privacy and comfort of their own home.

As the couple pass the threshold into the Intensification succession, the stimulation, both visual and physical, becomes more intimate, involving more intense physical arousal and even greater heights of pleasure requiring even greater self-control. The couple becomes much more physical, their passion becoming much more intense. This is the time for close physical interaction. Both individuals may lie on the convocation stone together as they intensify each other's sexual stimulation.

As the male is the Principal Conduit in this case, the priestess may position herself between the male's legs and, bending over the convocation stone, take his penis in her mouth, using her hands to caress his testicles, stomach, and nipples. She may also insert a phallus into the male's anus. Alternatively, the priestess may gently bite the nipples of the male as she masturbates his penis, or she may sit over the male in opposite direction, with her vagina just above the male's face, while she bends over and takes his penis in her mouth. This is a particularly good position for her to stimulate his anus with fingers or a phallus. At the same time the male may stimulate the priestess's vagina with mouth, fingers, and phallus.

Various methods and combinations of penetration, whether vaginal, anal, or oral, are also used at this stage by both priestess and the Principal Conduit.

These ideas are put forward simply to illustrate the level of intensity of the contact between the priestess and the Principal Conduit. Many other positions are possible, and there is a great variety of source materials from which these imaginative positions may be drawn. The point is that both individuals should be doing their utmost to ensure the maximum stimulation of the other.

There will be innumerable approaches to the threshold of the Quickening and the same amount of retreats until, eventually, the priestess decides to commit to the Quickening. Only the priestess may make the decision to take the Gathering to the next succession of the Projection Cycle.

It is worth remembering that we are focusing here only on the physical and sensual elements of the ritual. You must not forget the duality of the approaching orgasm and the need to recall and invoke your spell as explained in part 2.

The priestess and the Principal Conduit have now committed to the Quickening. This is the point at which the approaching orgasm in inevitable and very imminent. Hopefully, their impending orgasms have been synchronized by the cycle of repeatedly approaching and retreating from the threshold of the Quickening, so that when they both commit they may do so in a synchronized state.

As both parties commit to the Quickening, the priestess says:

"The Quickening is here!"

As soon as she has said this, both parties begin to chant the spell repeatedly, increasing in speed and volume as the orgasm approaches. It is possible for both parties to synchronize their orgasm by synchronizing their chanting of the spell.

If the pair is coupled when the priestess acknowledges the Quickening, they separate and lie together on the convocation stone to reach orgasm. They may augment each other's stimulation by continued contact but must never reach orgasm while coupled.

The arrival of the orgasm and the projection of the generated energy are

marked by the shouting of the spell as the energy is projected. The vocalization of the spell at high volume assists and magnifies the power of the Projection and the potency of the spell.

Once the Projection is complete and the orgasm subsides, it is the role of the priestess to maintain and fuel the generated energy's journey by further stimulation of the Principal Conduit. In the circumstances described here, that is, the priestess and the male Principal Conduit, the favored position for this continued stimulation is as mentioned above, with the priestess standing between the male's legs, stimulating the penis in her mouth and the testes and anus with her fingers. This is done gently and sympathetically so as not to distract the male during his visualized journey.

Once the Principal Conduit has "returned" from his journey, the parties separate.

Following the Relaxation succession, the male returns to his original place, seated on the ground facing the working stone, and the priestess stands in front of the working stone facing the center of the Circle.

The priestess now begins the group congress. Three times she chants the spell and the male repeats it. Then the priestess says:

"The spell is cast. The spell is bound. Let it run its course, and let no one interfere!"

This is the final part of the Projection Cycle and the confirmation of the spell.

If there are no other matters to be attended to within the protective Circle, the working stone candles are extinguished and the Circle is unsealed and erased. The ritual site is dismantled and the Gift left for nature as the participants depart the site.

You may have recognized that there are many opportunities for you to personalize the ritual, making it your own unique working and using your own individual phrases. The only governing factors, which deal with the more "spiritual" aspects of the ritual, have been emphasized both here and in part 2. Outside these imperatives, you are free to interpret the ritual in your own special way.

The Sex Magic Ritual: The Single Participant

There is absolutely no reason why sex magic cannot be used by the individual Druid or Druidess. I know a number of hedge Druids and Druidesses who practice solitary sex magic rituals on a regular basis. In fact, many Druids and Druidesses and members of Gatherings find it useful to conduct solitary rituals on occasion.

The biggest danger of solitary ritual practice, whether sex magic or another ritual, is the temptation to cut corners and leave out essential parts for the sake of convenience. This is purely a matter of self-discipline. If the ritual is not undertaken in its absolute and complete form, then its effectiveness is always compromised.

The solitary sex magic ritual begins with the same preparation as does the pair ritual. In this case, the individual is both priest or priestess and participant.

There is exactly the same need for clarity when crafting the spell or intention, and the same need for cleansing, purification, and energizing of the individual and the ritual tools and accessories to be used. The ritual site is laid out in the same manner, and the protective Circle is cast in exactly the same way.

As the individual enters the Circle for the ritual, he or she extends his or her arms so that the hands pass through the flames of the candles at each side of the entrance portal. This is a symbolic final purification act. Having done this, the individual seals the Circle in whichever fashion he or she chooses.

One advantage of the solitary ritual is that it may become the most creative and free-flowing of rituals, as it can be continually developed and improvised by the individual as he or she moves through the successions. Methods of exploiting each individual succession to best effect can be explored and crafted by the individual, while at the same time new and exciting means of stimulation may be incorporated.

There are two warnings to be given, however.

First, it is easy to become introverted and self-possessed when working rituals on your own. In the wrong environment or wrong state of mind, your actions may become obsessive and dangerous. Make the effort to constantly review your intentions and actions; try to stand outside yourself and see yourself within your environment. Reassess your relationships with other people and make sure that your rituals do not become the center of your life activities.

Second, it is usually more difficult to stimulate yourself than it is to be stimulated by others. Do not overemphasize your dependency on visual stimulation to the point of obsession. Pornography plays a valid role in all forms of sex magic, but do not let it become a major factor in your life. Remember your original intention: the desire to influence the collective energy through your own energy generated by your orgasm. Do not lose sight of this, or the ritual dissolves into an indulgence in shallow sexual gratification.

Once the Circle is sealed, you will move through the seven successions of the Projection Cycle as laid out in part 2, omitting only the social activities of libation. You will have to change roles at appropriate points in the ritual; you will also need to change your relative positions. All this, however, adds to your opportunity to be creative.

The ways and means you use to provide your own stimulation are limited only by your own imagination. The words you use during the ritual can be the same ones used in paired and group rituals, or they can be entirely of your own making.

At the end of the ritual, unseal and erase the Circle. Do not forget to undertake the Gift before you depart the ritual site.

Solitary rituals are useful in developing your maturity as a Druidic priest or priestess. They provide many opportunities for you to hone your skills and explore your craft. They are a means of exploring the sensory awareness of your body, in your own time; you can test the responses of your senses to different stimuli. Do not be tempted to simply masturbate to discover your most exciting erotic stimulus, as this focuses your attention solely upon your genital area. Try to involve as many of your senses as you can. Touch, smell, taste, sight, and hearing all have their place in erotic arousal. Simple masturbation is a perfect starting place but by this stage you should be trying to discover the previously unused sensual receptors of your body and taking yourself to new heights of arousal never before experienced.

THE SEX
MAGIC
RITUAL: THE
SINGLE
PARTICIPANT

217

The Sex Magic Ritual: The Group

The group ritual is potentially the most difficult form of sex magic to both organize and facilitate.

One of the more difficult tasks of the priest or priestess is ensuring partner balance at rituals. It is essential that there are adequate males present for those participants who prefer to interact with males and adequate females present for those who prefer to interact with females. Bearing in mind that all sex magic workings and rituals are totally participative, having surplus males or females either creates a small audience for those involved or puts undue pressure on particular males or females who end up with additional unwanted suitors. Neither is an ideal situation.

Planning this balance can be a very challenging activity, and even the best-laid plans can go astray if someone is taken ill or cannot attend the Gathering.

On a few, very rare occasions, a priestess may appoint herself the Principal Conduit and assemble a small (say two- to six-person) all-male Gathering. In this case all the male participants serve the wishes and desires of the priestess as she progresses through the Projection Cycle. A priest may convene a similar assembly with an all-female cast.

A balanced gender mix ensures a high level of participation at the Gatherings and also offers the most rewarding experience possible for each of the participants. It may well be the case that couples or pairs of individuals will choose to exchange partners or combine into larger groups, but these will always be balanced by the underlying mathematics of the equal gender balance.

You will find that as the Gathering divides into groups during the sex magic ritual, the practiced pairs mentioned earlier will be the basis for the formation of larger active groups. However, there must always be the opportunity for these pairs to participate between themselves, without any additional group members.

Just as in the ritual for the pair, the roles the individuals in the Gathering adopt often reflect their everyday sexual predilections. A sexually dominant individual will undoubtedly be attracted to submissive participants, and in the same way, the submissive participants will be attracted to him or her. The result will be small groups of submissive participants focusing their attention on a dominant male or female.

For the purpose of this example we will assume that a priestess is facilitating the ritual, the Principal Conduit is male, and the rest of the Gathering are male and female in equal proportion. You can then superimpose your own circumstances upon the workings as appropriate.

For this ritual you will need:

- **Your wand(s).** Used in all your rituals.

- **Your stave.** To cast your first Circle.

- **Your salt canister.** To cast your second Circle. Should contain sufficient salt for the purpose.

- **Your hand-held candle.** To cast your third Circle.

- **Your dagger.** To seal the Circle, along with the salt and candle above.

- **Your cauldron, filled with moon-cleansed water.** For the purification activities within the ritual.

- **Your chalice and libations goblets.** To hold and distribute your libations.

- **Your libations.** Liquid and baked libations for the Gathering.

- **Two floor-standing candleholders.** To create the portal within your Circle. The flames of these two candles will be at shoulder height.

- **Three working stone candles, in candleholders.** The center focus of your working stone.

- **Your phallus.** For stimulation during the ritual. Use a number of phalluses if you have them, together with the necessary condoms needed to ensure hygiene.

- **Your binding vessel.** Use only if you have created a binding vessel for this particular Gathering and all the participants who contributed donations of earth to the binding vessel are present.

- **Incense burners or essential oil evaporators.** To enhance the atmosphere of the ritual and invest the working with the attributes of the herbs used.

- **Cleansing cloths.** As many as you feel are necessary.

The ritual begins with the priestess raising her sensory awareness using the inverted triangular pyramid working. She then casts a triple-cast Circle of a suitable size. As each of the participants enters the Circle, they extend their arms to each side, level with their shoulders, passing each hand quickly through the flames of the two portal candles, a symbolic final purification of the body. Once all are inside the Circle, the priestess seals the Circle with the triple seal. The participants are now enclosed within the protective Circle and are ready to begin the sex magic ritual.

The priestess stands in front of the working stone, facing the Gathering, and says:

"You are welcome among friends. May each welcome the other as we gather here together."

As this is said, the participants of the Gathering mingle, greeting each other with a handshake, hug, or whatever gesture feels comfortable at the time. The priestess also walks among the Gathering and greets everyone in the same way. She then returns to the working stone.

The participants of the Gathering (including the Principal Conduit) sit on the ground facing the working stone.

The priestess stands before the working stone and brings the first of the candles, the collective energy candle, to the front of the stone. She lights the candle, raises it into the air, and says:

"As this flame burns, so we converge with the collective energy. Our energies mingle, our potential becomes one."

The "flame of the collective energy" candle is placed at the back, in the center, of the working stone.

The priestess then lights the sun, or male, candle, holds it up, and says:

"As this flame burns it bind us with the sun. We invoke the sun's influence upon our workings."

The "flame of the sun" candle is placed to the left and slightly forward of the "flame of the collective energy" candle.

She then lights the third and final moon or female candle, holds it up, and says:

"As this flame burns I bind myself with the moon. I invoke the moon's influence upon all I do."

The "flame of the moon" candle is placed to the right and slightly in front of the "flame of the collective energy" candle, forming the candle triangle.

You will see that this third invocation is a personal one. If the ritual is facilitated by the male, then the moon candle is lit before the sun candle, and this same personal invocation is given for the sun candle.

With all three candle flames lit, the priestess stands before them at the front/center of the working stone and extends her arms out so that each of her palms is directly above each of the sun and moon flames, close enough to feel the heat of the flames without burning her palms. She then brings both hands together above the central collective energy flame to form a "cup" shape above the flame, saying:

"I unite all things with the collective energy, as in nature they belong. I offer myself to this union, together with all those present here. Unite us in your common bond."

This opening part of the ritual, called the "uniting of the flames," is now complete.

If the Gathering has a previously crafted binding vessel, the priestess now lifts it aloft, saying:

"This binding vessel binds all present to one. I now bind it to the united flames as a symbol of our affinity."

She passes the binding vessel quickly through each of the three flames, then places it in the center of the candle triangle, at the base of the "flame of the collective energy" candle. As we have seen previously, the center point of a triangle is a power point.

The preparation of the working stone is now complete.

The next step of the ritual is the giving and receiving of the first libation. The first libation is a liquid one, usually a mixture of metheglin and poteen. Some Gatherings use mead or a mixture of mead and poteen; others use wine, cider, ale, or whatever is favored by the participants. The advantage of metheglin is that it can be fermented with whatever herbs, spices, and flowers you feel have the appropriate attributes for your working. Whichever libation is chosen, an amount sufficient for all the participants is placed in the chalice before the ritual starts.

The libation may be served cold or warm. To warm the libation, follow the directions in part 1.

The priestess positions the chalice and a number of libation goblets at the front and center of the working stone. With her hands on either side of the chalice, she says:

"To welcome all here I offer this libation."

Taking the chalice ladle, she ladles a small amount of the libation into one of the libations goblets. Raising the goblet into the air with both hands, she says:

"What we have taken from the earth, we share with the earth. Whatever we take to ourselves we return threefold."

Having said this, she pours the contents of the goblet onto the ground in three successive parts.

The priestess then fills sufficient goblets with the libation and they are passed among the participants of the Gathering, each of whom takes his or her fill. There need not be a separate goblet for each participant. If the goblets are of a normal size, one goblet will contain sufficient libation for three participants. If the goblets run dry before all have had their fill, they can be returned to the priestess and refilled.

The priestess retains one goblet for herself and drinks her libation from it.

The goblets are returned to the priestess, who wipes them quickly with a cleansing cloth and returns them to the working stone.

The priestess must now prepare the convocation stone to receive the Principal Conduit.

Picking up her wand in her right hand (or in her left if she is left-handed), the priestess moves to the convocation stone. Extending her wand above the stone, she walks around it three times, saying quietly to herself:

"I invoke only what is good, I intend only what is beneficial, I banish all that is unwelcome."

The priestess then returns to the working stone, picks up the cauldron with the moon-cleansed water, and returns to the convocation stone. Again she walks three times around the stone, but this time she dips the tip of the wand into the water and sprinkles drops of it on the stone as she walks. She again says:

"I invoke only what is good, I intend only what is beneficial, I banish all that is unwelcome."

She returns the cauldron to the working stone and stands with her back to it, facing the center of the Circle. She says, in a loud voice:

"Come forward who wishes to lie here."

The Principal Conduit approaches the priestess and says:

"That is I."

The priestess says:

"And are you named?"

If the Principal Conduit has already been named, then his name is spoken. We shall use the name "David" for the sake of this example.

The Principal Conduit (David) says:

"Yes, my name is David. I wish to lie here."

The priestess says:

"Then as I know your name to be David, take your place as it is offered."

David then takes his place on the convocation stone, with his head at the center point of the Circle and his feet facing the working stone. This means that he is lying in the south/north orientation, so the energies will flow through him from his head to his feet, aiding the projection of generated energy from his body.

The priestess now stands between the two stones, facing the center of the Circle, and says:

"I welcome all those that wish us well. We are gathered with the intention of creating change. Change that offers benefit and goodwill. Our spell is crafted and I offer it to you."

She then speaks the spell for the first time. The Gathering already knows the spell and will have committed it to memory. For the sake of simplicity we shall just call it "the spell."

The priestess says:

"The spell."

The Principal Conduit repeats the spell three times:

"The spell; the spell; the spell."

The priestess, picking up her wand and cauldron, walks to the convocation stone where the Principal Conduit now lies and says:

"Our Principal Conduit is David. Through him we shall cast and bind our spell."

She sprinkles the Principal Conduit with the moon-cleansed water, using her wand to do so. As she does this, she says:

"I anoint you, David, and commit my efforts to your internal energy."

The cauldron and the wand are placed back on the working stone and a second libation is given and taken in the same way as the first.

The priestess faces the center of the Circle and says:

"Now we begin our work. We seek to awaken that which is within us."

Now the Projection Cycle begins. At this point the Gathering divides into various subgroups. The most important group gathers around the Principal Conduit lying on the convocation stone. These are the priestess's chosen assistants who will help her lead the Principal Conduit through the seven successions, in addition to stimulating the priestess and each other as they progress to their own orgasms. The other participants in the Gathering form pairs or groups as they wish.

The progression of the Gathering passes through the Awakening, Augmentation, and Intensification in much the same way as described above in the paired

PERFORMING

WORKINGS

AND RITUALS

ritual. The priestess, her assistants, and the Principal Conduit focus on each other, and the other members of the Gathering focus on the individuals they have paired or grouped with. When the priestess deems it fitting for the ritual to progress from one succession to another, she says:

"I am content. Let us progress to the next succession."

The purpose of these announcements is the beginning of the synchronization of the Gathering's sexual arousal. Bear in mind that it is the intention of the whole Gathering to reach orgasm at the same moment and thereby to maximize the projection of the generated energy by adding to it their own internal energy. To help synchronize everyone's efforts, the priestess exercises control over the pace of the progression through the successions.

When the time comes for the priestess to commit to the Quickening, she says:

"The Quickening is here!"

As soon as she has said this, the focus of the Gathering concentrates on the Principal Conduit. All the participants in the Gathering begin to chant the spell repeatedly, increasing the speed and volume as they approach orgasm. It is possible for the participants in the Gathering to synchronize their orgasm by synchronizing their chanting of the spell.

If any of the participants are coupled when the priestess acknowledges the Quickening, they separate and lie or stand together to reach orgasm. They may augment each other's stimulation by continued contact but must never reach orgasm while coupled. It is usual for all the participants and the priestess to face north (toward the working stone) as they orgasm; this places them in the same orientation as the Principal Conduit, augmenting the power and potency of his Projection.

The arrival of the orgasm and the projection of the generated energy are marked by the shouting of the spell by the entire Gathering as the energy is projected. The vocalization of the spell at high volume assists and magnifies the power of the Projection and the potency of the spell.

Once the Projection is complete and the orgasm subsides, it is the role of the priestess and her attendants to maintain and fuel the generated energy's journey

by further stimulation of the male Principal Conduit, as described in the paired ritual above. The paired individuals and smaller groups within the Gathering fuel and support their dominant member in the same manner.

Once the Principal Conduit and the other individuals experiencing the visualized journey have "returned," all parties separate.

Following the Relaxation succession, all participants, including the Principal Conduit, return to their original places, seated on the ground facing the working stone, and the priestess stands in front of the working stone facing the center of the Circle.

The priestess now begins the group congress. Three times she chants the spell and the Gathering repeat it. Then the priestess says:

"The spell is cast. The spell is bound. Let it run its course, and let no one interfere!"

This is the final part of the Projection Cycle and the confirmation of the spell. The priestess then says:

"Our work is done. Let us bond our friendship and trust in each other with this final libation."

The final liquid libation is undertaken in the same manner as the previous two.

On this occasion a baked libation is also given and taken after the liquid libation has been distributed. The priestess holds a part of the libation—a baked loaf of bread, a cake, or whatever baked good has been provided—in the air, saying:

"What we have taken from the earth, we share with the earth. Whatever we take to ourselves we return threefold."

Having said this, she breaks a small piece from the loaf and drops it onto the ground, then does so again a second and third time. The remainder of the loaf and the other baked libations are then distributed among the Gathering.

As the participants in the Gathering consume the libation, the priestess gives them a gift in the form of a spoken piece of wisdom or knowledge; it is intended to feed their internal energy as the libation feeds their physical body. The

A small Gathering around the Principal Conduit, shown in this case as a female, in the early stages of the Ritual. The spell is spoken for the first time and then repeated three times by the Principal Conduit as the other participants enhance her energy.

subject matter of this wisdom is entirely the choice of the priestess, but it would ideally relate to the content of the spell just projected.

If there are no other matters to be attended to within the protective Circle, the working stone candles are extinguished and the Circle is unsealed and erased. The ritual site is dismantled and the Gift left for nature as the participants depart the site.

This then completes the sex magic ritual for the assembled Gathering. As you can see, it bears close resemblance to the ritual facilitated for the paired couple, which is not surprising, as the same intentions are involved.

When the Rituals End

"And so we scatter . . ."

When you are planning your rituals, it is important that you spend time and energy on ways to make sure that the ritual does not just fade away, and that it has a very positive and inspiring ending. Everyone involved in your ritual should feel uplifted and energized by the experience.

Make sure that as the participants leave the Circle there are well-understood arrangements for them to access their clothing and belongings. There is nothing worse than standing naked in the cold, having just expended a large amount of your physical and mental energy, not being able to find something warm to put on.

Encourage your Gathering to stay and chat awhile after the ritual, to express their feelings about the activities and get to know each other even better. Use this time to plan the time, date, and location of your next Gathering or to confirm future contact arrangements.

This is a time when most of your Gathering will be feeling very good in the afterglow of the ritual. Use this precious time to express positive reinforcement of their individual efforts, answer any questions they may have, or address any concerns that may be worrying them.

Once your participants have left, take a few quiet moments on your own to assess and evaluate your own efforts and commitment while it is still fresh in your mind. Place yourself in the shoes of your participants and ask yourself what your opinion of yourself would be if you were they. A little self-criticism is usually a very good thing, and you can base part of your development and future training on the outcome of your self-evaluation.

Last Thoughts

In writing this book I have discovered a massive amount about myself. The necessary research has required that I revisit many of the places I frequented when I was young and search out many old associates whom I had not seen or spoken to in years. It reminded me of who I was as a youth, and it made me realize who I am now.

I hope that, in some small way, reading this book may be as productive an experience for you as writing it has been for me.

I firmly believe that there is a place for true Druidism and its inseparable values in our modern world. In fact, I prove it every day by my mere existence. My life revolves around the principles I have briefly described in this book, and I know that they work.

Sex magic is one of the most powerful tools in the Druid's possession. Enjoy it. Use it well and with only good intentions and you will benefit as I have from the knowledge you gain.